The Teacher Development Series

Uncovering Grammar

Scott Thornbury

MACMILLAN
HEINEMANN
English Language Teaching

Macmillan Heinemann English Language Teaching
Between Towns Road, Oxford OX4 3PP
A division of Macmillan Publishers Limited
Companies and representatives throughout the world

ISBN 0 333 95282 0

First published 2001

Designed by eMC Design
Commissioned illustrations by:
Dave Pattison, Jim Peacock, Clyde Pearson, Andy Warrington, Geoff Waterhouse

The author and publishers wish to thank the following who have kindly granted permission
to use copyright material:

Atlantic Syndication Partners on behalf of the *Evening Standard* newspaper for an extract from a news item
published 10th July, 2000; Faber and Faber Ltd. for a quote from Choruses from *The Rock* by T.S. Eliot,
included in *Collected Poems 1909–1962* (1963); Grimsby and Scunthorpe Newspapers Ltd. for two news
items published in the *Grimsby Telegraph*; HSBC Holdings plc for an extract from the leaflet *Watch Your Cards*
(October, 1992); The Industrial Society *Navigating Complexity* by Arthur Battram 1988, p51; Kingfisher
Publications plc for the extract 'Meteor' from *Kingfisher Pocket Encyclopedia* edited by A. Jack (1983); Little,
Brown & Co. (UK) for a short extract from *The Quark and the Jaguar: Adventures in the Simple and the
Complex*, by Murray Gell-Mann (1995); Lowe Lintas Advertising Agency and Vauxhall Motors for an
advertisement of the Astra GTE Convertible car; Market House Books Ltd. for an extract from *Who's Who in
the Twentieth Century* edited by Asa Briggs (1999); National Centre for English Language Teaching and
Research, Australia, for the dialogue extract from 'The language teacher as decision maker' by D. Nunan in
The Second Language Curriculum In Action edited by Geoff Brindley © Macquarie University (1990); News
International Syndication for the article 'Love takes flight' by Robin Young in *The Times*, 5th June, 1993, ©
Times Newspapers Limited; Oxford University Press for an extract from 'Maximising learning potential in
the communicative classroom' by Kumaravadivelu in *English Language Teaching Journal*, Vol. 47, No. 1, pp
12–21 (1993); Palgrave Publishers Ltd. for an extract from 'Effects of task repetition: appraising the
developing language of learners' from *Challenge and Change in Language Teaching* edited by J. and D. Willis,
published by Heinemann (1996); Pearson Education Ltd. for the item 'grammar' from *Active Study
Dictionary* and for an extract from *Language Teaching Methodology* by D. Nunan, published by Prentice Hall
(1991); Penguin Books Australia Ltd. for two quotes from *The Penguin Book of Australian Jokes* by Philip
Adams and Patrice Newell (1994); The Random House Group for the poem 'Walking at Dusk' from *Silence
in the Snowy Fields* by Robert Bly, published by Jonathan Cape Ltd. 1955 and 1967; Rogers, Coleridge &
White Ltd, London, on behalf of Stephen Pile for extracts from *The Book of Heroic Failures* copyright ©
Stephen Pile, 1979; SmartGroups Marketing for their advertisement published in *The Guardian*, 19th June,
2000; Virgin Publishing Ltd. for the extract 'Nowt Taken Out' from *Urban Myths* by Phil Healey and Rick
Glanville (1996).

Whilst every effort has been made to locate the owners of copyright, in some cases this has been
unsuccessful. The publishers apologise for any infringement or failure to acknowledge the original sources
and will be glad to include any necessary correction in subsequent printings.

The authors and publishers would like to thank the following for permission to reproduce their
photographs: Science Photo Library (front cover); Stone, p47

Printed and bound in Great Britain by Scotprint

2005 2004 2003 2002 2001
10 9 8 7 6 5 4 3 2 1

Contents

About the author

I work in Barcelona, where I divide my time between teacher training and writing. I also serve on a number of boards under the UCLES CILTS schemes. I have taught and trained teachers in Egypt, the UK and New Zealand, as well as in Spain. I have an MA in TEFL from the University of Reading, as well as the RSA/UCLES Diploma. I have been involved in a number of course book projects, as well as having written three books on the subject of language teaching (including this one). I am presently writing a book on vocabulary, co-writing one on conversation, as well as co-editing a book on critical pedagogy.

Thanks

This book, like its subject, more or less emerged, and I can't always trace to their source all the tributaries that have fed into it. Books and articles that have influenced me are mentioned in footnotes. But it's often been the conference workshops and short courses I've attended that have been more memorable, and hence more formative. For that reason, I particularly want to record my debt to Diane Larsen-Freeman, Peter Skehan, Rod Ellis, Leo van Lier, Martin Bygate, Dick Schmidt, Paul Nation, and Rob Batstone. (Of course, no blame should be attached to any of them for my uptake of their input.)

Closer to home, much chewing-of-fat with my workmates at International House, Barcelona, has helped uncover and scaffold my argument. For the same reason, I want to thank the members of the 'Dogme' discussion group – a truly emergent phenomenon. And a big thank you to Oliver and his class for their part in the process. The final product owes to the initiative, encouragement and insights of both Jill Florent (my commissioning editor) and Adrian Underhill (my series editor), as well as to the generous enthusiasm of Jim Scrivener and Tim Bowen, and to the truly inspired editorship of Alyson Maskell. To all of them my sincere thanks.

Dedication

For the staff and students of IH Alexandria, 1980–85.

> *"It goes on being Alexandria still."*

The Teacher Development Series

TEACHER DEVELOPMENT is the process of becoming the best teacher you can be. It means becoming a student of learning, your own as well as that of others.

It represents a widening of the focus of teaching to include not only the subject matter and the teaching methods, but also the people who are working with the subject and using the methods. It means taking a step back to see the larger picture of what goes on in learning and how the relationship between students and teachers influences learning. It also means attending to small details which can in turn change the bigger picture. Teacher development is a continuous process of transforming human potential into human performance, a process that is never finished.

The Teacher Development Series offers perspectives on learning that embrace topic, method and person as parts of one larger interacting whole. We aim to help you, the teacher, trainer or academic manager to stretch your awareness not only of what you do and how you do it, but also of how you affect your learners and colleagues. This will enable you to extract more from your own experience, both as it happens and in retrospect, and to become more actively involved in your own continuous learning. The books themselves will focus on new treatments of familiar subjects as well as areas that are just emerging as subjects of the future.

The series represents work that is in progress rather than finished or closed. The authors are themselves exploring, and invite you to bring your own experience to the study of these books while at the same time learning from the experiences of others. We encourage you to observe, value and understand your own experience, and to evaluate and integrate relevant external practice and knowledge into your own internal evolving model of effective teaching and learning.

Adrian Underhill

Other titles in the Teacher Development Series

Children Learning English	Jayne Moon
Learning Teaching	Jim Scrivener
The Language Teacher's Voice	Alan Maley
Readings in Teacher Development	Katie Head and Pauline Taylor
Inside Teaching	Tim Bowen and Jonathan Marks
Sound Foundations	Adrian Underhill
The ELT Manager's Handbook	Graham Impey and Nic Underhill

Introduction to *Uncovering Grammar*

Out of the slimy mud of words, out of the sleet and hail of verbal imprecisions...
There spring the perfect order of speech, and the beauty of incantation. (T.S. Eliot)

This is a book about grammar, but not so much a book about how to teach grammar as a book about how grammar is learned. There is a difference. I can teach you the subjunctive in Spanish – its forms and rules of use – and I can even do it with flair, humour, brilliance and insight. But this is no guarantee that you are going to learn it. You may remember me, the teacher, and the circumstances of the lesson. You may even remember some facts about the subjunctive itself. Traces of that memory of those facts may get you through the end-of-year exam. But, placed in a situation of real language use, can you access the subjunctive? Unlikely.

As second language learners we've all had that experience: fumbling an order for coffee in Portuguese or a timetable enquiry in Chinese. (After six years of school French I recently ordered a beer in a French café and got two, thanks to a poorly installed article system!) And yet a great deal of teaching carries on as if these language embarrassments were simply freak occurrences and still assumes that *I teach, you learn.*

This book takes a different line. It looks at grammar not as an 'out there' body of language facts that have to be forced into the learner like stuffing into a chicken. Rather it assumes that grammar is a kind of organic process that, in the right conditions, grows of its own accord and in its own mysterious way. The key to success – and the indispensable role of the teacher – is providing those conditions.

So, this is a book about grammar, but definitely not about *covering* grammar in the traditional sense of 'Today's Tuesday so we're going to do the present perfect'. Nor is it a book primarily about *discovering* grammar – by means of language awareness activities, although awareness-raising certainly comes into it. Nor is it a book about *recovering* grammar – from where it has allegedly been side-lined by the so-called communicative approach. Rather, it is a book about *uncovering* grammar – letting the grammar out, placing one's trust in the emergent properties of language.

In Chapter 1 we take a look at the role grammar plays in 'perfecting' language, and I will argue that grammar is better considered as a dynamic *process* – for which we lack an adequate verb in English, although attempts have been made to supply one. In Chapter 2 I will suggest some activity types that may activate the 'grammaring' process.

Grammar processing ability may be acquired simply by hanging out with speakers of the language and wanting to sound like them. However, few learners have the time nor the motivation to trust to nature like this. Instead, they look to teachers to help them along and to cut corners. In Chapter 3 we look at ways that teachers can intervene in the acquisition of process grammar, and, specifically, at the role of feedback and attention.

In Chapter 4 I put the case for regarding grammar as an emergent process. Such a view calls for a rethink of classroom instruction. This does not invalidate the role of the teacher: on the contrary, the teacher plays a key role in the process of grammaring – but it is a role more facilitative than pedantic, more reactive than pre-emptive. In Chapter 5 we take a wider look at the implications of a process grammar view and conclude with some hints as to how a product approach to grammar and a process approach might be merged.

In Part 2 you will find a number of photocopiable worksheets, with suggestions as to how they may be used, in order to put into practice some of the ideas in the book. But, remember, your best resource is yourself and your learners – and the interaction between you. Make discourse your resource: nothing more is needed in order to free the grammar.

Chapter 1   **Grammar as process**

Is grammar a *thing* or is it something that *happens*? This chapter will argue that maybe it is a bit of both. When we describe language, as in the *grammar of English*, grammar is more noun-like than verb-like. It is a body of facts about the language: 'The present perfect is formed by the auxiliary *have* plus the past participle', etc. On the other hand, when we *use* language in real communication, grammar manifests itself in ways that seem to have little to do with the conscious application of these linguistic facts. Grammar seems to be more like a process, whereby shades of meaning are mapped on to basic ideas. It is a process for which we need a verb – something like *grammaring*. The verb-iness of grammar, then, is the subject of this chapter: grammar as a *doing* word.

Grammar, grammars and grammaring

According to this dictionary definition[1], there are at least two senses of the word *grammar*. Language teaching is generally concerned with the former – uncountable – meaning of grammar. That is, grammar as a system of rules (or patterns) which describe the formation of a language's sentences. (But note that this definition will be reworked in Chapter 4, to take into account the *learner's* grammar.)

> **grammar** /ˈgræmər/ n **1** [U] (the study and use of) rules by which words change their forms and are combined into sentences: *I find German grammar very difficult.* | *You must try to improve your grammar.* **2** [C] a book which teaches these rules: *This is the best Italian grammar I've seen.*

You'll note that, according to the dictionary definition here, grammar in both its senses is a *noun*: a grammar, your grammar, etc. Nevertheless, the focus of this first chapter is to argue that grammar is in fact a *verb*. Or, at least, that there should be a verb *to grammar*, to go along with the noun *grammar*. Just as there is a verb *to rain* to go along with the noun *rain*. Or *to walk* and *a walk*.

In other words, grammar is not simply a thing. It is also something that you *do*. Or (as we shall be arguing later) something that – in certain conditions – *happens*.

To use an analogy: an omelette is the product of a (relatively simple but skilful) process involving the beating and frying of eggs. The process and the product are clearly two quite different things, and we could call one *making an omelette* (or even *'omeletting'*) and the other *an omelette*. Similarly, the grammar that a linguist might identify in a statement like *If I'd known you were coming, I would have baked a cake* or *Mary had a little lamb* is the result of a process – in this case an invisible mental one. Again, we need to maintain a distinction between the product and its processes of creation.

To take the analogy one step further: to someone who had never seen an omelette being made, it might be difficult to infer the process from the product. They would be seriously mistaken if they thought that making an omelette was simply a case of taking a lot of little bits of omelette and sticking them together. So, too, with grammar. What you see and how it came to be that way are two quite different things. It would be naïve to suppose that the fluid production of a sentence like *If I'd known you were coming, I would have baked a cake* results from the cumulative sticking together of individual words or even of individual grammatical structures. The same goes for the way we learn languages in the first place. Inferring the process of language acquisition from its product (grammar) is like inferring the process of 'omeletting' from the omelette. Or, for that matter, inferring the chicken from the egg.

Yet a basic assumption behind a great deal of language teaching is exactly that: if you teach the product, the process will take care of itself. 'This is an omelette. I cut it in bits. You can see what it looks like from the inside. OK. Are you ready? Now make one!' This is what I call the 'Humpty Dumpty Fallacy'. Just to remind you:

> All the King's horses and all the King's men
> Couldn't put Humpty together again.

The language teaching equivalent is: I, the teacher, will cut the language into lots of little pieces – called *grammar* – so that you, the learner, will be able to reassemble them in real communication. Thus: conjunction *if* + subject pronoun + past perfect (consisting of past auxiliary *had* + past participle), followed by nominal *that*-clause, consisting of... etc, etc. What happens, of course, is that learners take these little bits of grammar description and try to stick them together, and then wonder why they can't produce sentences like *If I'd known you were coming, I would have baked a cake*. It ignores the fact that the product and the process are two quite different things – that there is *grammar* and there is *grammaring*, and the latter is not easily inferable from the former. In short, a description of used language is not the same as language being used.

So, whereas *grammar* (uncountable) is the rules that describe language, and *a grammar* (countable) is a book containing these descriptions, both these meanings represent a product view of grammar. What this chapter – indeed this book – will argue, is that we need to combine this with a *process* view of grammar. In short, we need new metaphors for grammar.

Discovery activity

Here are some more metaphors that have been used about *grammar*. What assumptions underly them? How useful could they be?
1 Grammar is the *glue* that holds language together.
2 Grammar is the *engine* that drives language.
3 Grammar is a *map* of the language.
4 Grammar is *hard-wired* in the brain.
5 Grammar is both *particles* and *waves*.
6 Grammar is the *highway code* of language.

Can you add any others?

Commentary ■ ■ ■

Most teachers I have done this task with make reference to the cohesive and structural nature of grammar. Grammar is language's *glue, mortar, bones, building blocks, foundations,* etc, suggesting that without it the language falls apart or collapses. Such teachers view the teaching of grammar as an essential, often preliminary, stage: 'It's the structure on which you hang the rest of the language.' The image of grammar as a machine, or an *engine*, generating language, is a suggestive one and attests to grammar's creative and productive function. One teacher compared grammar to the body's DNA: 'It carries the code of language so that an infinite number of sentences can be produced and understood.' Others see grammar as a set of rules or prescriptions (*a map, guide book, highway code*). Such metaphors lend themselves to a prescriptive view of language teaching: 'It's what you should know if you want to speak correctly.'

Teachers and coursebook writers commonly talk about grammar as a series of *items* or *points*: an 'atomic particle' view of language. Such a view is ideal if you have to parcel the language up for teaching purposes. A different set of metaphors derives from the patterned and interconnected nature of grammar: that it ripples through the language in *waves*, or that it is a *network*. One teacher likened grammar to the *Dance of Shiva*: 'the image of the god's rhythmic activity as the source of all movement in the cosmos – and in language'. As we shall see in Chapter 4, this metaphor fits comfortably with a view of grammar as a complex, adaptive and emergent phenomenon. ■

Grammar in action

Let's have a look at a bit of language in action. Here is an exchange between two people having breakfast together. Your job is to identify the grammar.

A Coffee?
B Please.
A Milk? Sugar?
B No milk. One sugar.
       Thanks.
A Toast?
B No thanks.
A Juice?
B Mmm.

Not much grammar, is there? At least, not much grammar of a conventional kind. There are no verbs, for a start, so there are no verb endings (work*s*, work*ed*, work*ing*), a feature of grammar we commonly associate with highly inflected languages such as Spanish or Turkish. (This area of grammar is known as *morphology* – literally, the study of forms.) And, in the dialogue, each person's utterances (you can hardly call them sentences) are one word, at the most two words, long. So there is not much of the grammar of word order either – what is called *syntax*. In other words, there is little or no grammar of the morphological or syntactical kind. In fact, this exchange operates almost entirely on the word (or what is called *lexical*) level.

(Of course, intonation has an important part to play too. Consider the difference in meaning between *Juice* ⬇ and *Juice* ⬆.)

It would seem, therefore, that for certain kinds of communication, grammar takes a back seat. Later on we will look at why this is so. But first, let's see what happens when we put the grammar back in. Compare this exchange with the first one:

A Would you like some of this coffee?
B Yes, I would like some of that coffee, please.
A Do you take milk? Do you take sugar?
B I don't take milk. But I will take one sugar, thanks.
A Would you like some of this toast?
B I'd prefer not to have any of that toast, thanks.
A Can I offer you some of this juice?
B Yes, I would like some of that juice.

Does this strike you as unnecessarily wordy and even pedantic? In fact, it's the sort of conversation you might find in an old-fashioned coursebook. Not only do the speakers seem excessively polite, but B's answers, in particular, seem repetitive and redundant. Moreover, they often seem to be using words where, in real life, a gesture would do the job just as well. It's as if the conversation were taking place between two excessively polite and partially-sighted people. As we shall see, there is a close connection between grammar and formality, on the one hand, and between grammar and context, on the other.

Language without grammar

But before we look more closely at how grammar relates to context factors, let's go back to 'grammarless' language. We said that, for certain kinds of communication, grammar seems to be almost redundant. But for what kinds of communication? Well, consider the following. Why are they all light on grammar?

1 NO PARKING
2 THREE SHARE LOTTERY FORTUNE
3 'Tickets, please.'
4 'Annie, Sunday then. See you there. Tell Jack. Tom.'

Like the *Coffee? Please* conversation, all of these short texts are very thin on grammar. We will take each in turn and show how they support a view of language and of language learning that sees grammar as a process – or, to be more precise, a linguistic procedure for dealing with *distance*.

1 NO PARKING

There are clearly strong practical reasons for keeping this message as short as possible. 'You are kindly requested not to park here' would occupy too much space on a sign to be visible at any distance. (Although I once saw a road sign in New York that read 'Don't even THINK of parking here!') The de-grammared nature of public signs and notices does mean that at times they are unintentionally ambiguous, as in these examples:

SLOW CHILDREN CROSSING

DOOR ALARMED

HUMP

Ambiguities like these suggest that operating on the purely lexical (word) level may have its problems. In the days when people still sent telegrams (which are good examples of language that has been pared of its grammar), the potential for ambiguity was often exploited. Cary Grant is alleged to have found, on his agent's desk, a telegram from a reporter that asked HOW OLD CARY GRANT? Not wishing his age to be divulged, he telegramed back OLD CARY GRANT OK, HOW YOU?

2 THREE SHARE LOTTERY FORTUNE

This is recognizably a newspaper headline, and headlines, like road signs, are highly constrained by the need to pack a lot of meaning into the shortest possible space. THREE PEOPLE HAVE EACH WON A SHARE OF A FORTUNE IN THE NATIONAL LOTTERY is more grammatical but it doubles the length of the headline, without adding anything that couldn't have been inferred, or that won't be dealt with in the story that follows. Typically, the first sentence of the story itself is the grammatical version of the headline, in which the meaning is 'unpacked' for the reader:

> SURFER SURVIVES WHITE POINTER SHARK ATTACK
>
> A South Australian teenager has been attacked by a white pointer shark - and lived to tell the tale. Student Jason Bates, 17, suffered only minor cuts...
>
> *Adelaide Advertiser*

Headlines, by virtue of being 'de-grammared', are also subject to different readings[2]:

AIR FORCE CONSIDERS DROPPING SOME NEW WEAPONS

JERK INJURES NECK, WINS AWARD

CITY'S FIRST MAYOR TO BE BORN IN CUBA

DEFENDANT'S SPEECH ENDS IN LONG SENTENCE

WOMAN OFF TO JAIL FOR SEX WITH BOYS

But these are the exceptions. Normally, as with road signs, the reader doesn't have too much trouble 'unpacking' headlines. The words that have been taken out (such as articles and auxiliary verbs) carry little in the way of what is called 'propositional meaning'. Propositions (ie the main ideas) are typically encoded in nouns, verbs, adjectives, etc. Grammatical words, on the other hand, function to knit the propositions (ie the main ideas) together. When nouns are left out of headlines (as, for instance 'people' in THREE SHARE LOTTERY FORTUNE) the reader's common sense fills in the gap. The writer of the headline assumes a level of shared knowledge about lotteries that makes it unnecessary to spell out the details. Only a reader unfamiliar with what lotteries are and who wins them would be wondering 'Three what? Retired postmen? Sheep dogs?'

Discovery activity

What is missing from these headlines? What knowledge does the writer assume is shared?

TWO DIE AS MOB ATTACKS JAPANESE TOUR GROUP

ETON BOY EXPELLED AFTER MAY DAY PROTEST ARREST

MEN NOW LIVING FIVE YEARS LONGER

COCKROACH CAPABLE OF FEELING PAIN, SAYS STUDY

GAME PARK ANIMALS KILLED 'FOR FUN'

Commentary ■ ■ ■

An expanded version of each of these headlines would include the missing articles (*a mob, an Eton boy, the cockroach,* etc) as well as the auxiliary verbs and the verb *to be* (*men now are living... an Eton boy has been expelled... the cockroach is capable...*). Also some 'taken-for-granted' content words and clause elements have been left out (*two people die... Men are now living five years longer than they used to...*). Notice that, in these last two examples, the writer is assuming shared knowledge: that tour groups consist of people, and that average life expectancies are often compared with past averages. An alternative, but less likely, reading might be that *men are now living five years longer than women*, so the headline is not entirely unambiguous. The final headline is ambiguous, since it is not clear whether *killed* forms part of an active or a passive verb phrase. However, if it is an active verb it is in the past, suggesting a reference to a specific incident, which somehow seems unlikely. (Compare GAME PARK ANIMALS KILL 'FOR FUN': the use of the present sets up an expectation that the article is a report of a scientific study.) ■

3 'Tickets, please'

Because a lot of language use takes place in fairly routine and predictable situations, we are used to assuming a high degree of shared knowledge with other speakers. This in turn means that there is little need to be very explicit. It explains why ticket collectors can get away with requests like 'Tickets, please' or even 'Tickets'. Passengers on buses or trains are already in a context which primes them to fill in the gaps ('Can you show me your tickets, please?'). It is unlikely that they would fill the gap with 'Have you seen my tickets?' or 'What is the French for tickets?', inferences that might be quite plausible in different contexts.

By the same token, passengers on a bus would be hard pressed to make sense of the ticket collector saying 'scalpel', whereas an assistant surgeon in an operating theatre would be able to make perfect sense of it. In other words, the context creates shared expectations that reduce the need for language, and for grammar in particular. Just as we saw with the *Coffee? Please* conversation, when speakers are referring to things that are in the immediate physical context, words, intonation and gesture are often enough to convey meanings precisely and unambiguously.

When the references contained in the propositions extend beyond the immediate context, however, lexical language becomes less effective. This is where we need to start enlisting grammar. Imagine, for example, the surgeon has left the scalpel at home, and phones home for it. 'Scalpel!' will no longer do. It makes too many assumptions regarding the state of the listener's shared knowledge. (It also will come across as rather impolite if the person who answers the phone is not a close family member or friend: more on politeness later.) The surgeon will need to flesh the message out along the lines of 'Can you bring the scalpel I left next to the clock on the mantelpiece over to the hospital fairly quickly?' And, if no one is at home and the surgeon has to leave a message on the answerphone, the message will be more complicated still.

We can illustrate these contextual layers quite simply like this:

Diagram 1

Diagram 2

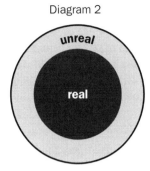

Diagram 1
As we move from the immediate space-time context to the distant space-time context, we create the need for more grammar.

Diagram 2
There is another kind of distance: the difference between the real and the unreal. Imagine the surgeon never had a scalpel but wants to express the wish for one: *If only I had a scalpel... If I had a scalpel I would...*

Hypothetical (or unreal) meaning creates a kind of cognitive distance and requires more grammar work. The two kinds of context (space-time and reality) can, of course, be combined: *He wished he'd had a scalpel yesterday...*

We can thus draw a simple rule-of-thumb: the more context, the more shared knowledge, and hence the less need for grammar. The bigger the knowledge 'gap', the more need for grammar. A good example of how this works in practice is in the exchanges between air traffic controllers and pilots, examples of which are given in an article by Mell[3]. Normally, these exchanges are of a very routine and linguistically simple nature:

> Pilot: Paris. Good afternoon. Jetset 762. Level 370. On course Deauville.

Despite the physical distance separating speaker and listener, the knowledge gap is very narrow: the content and form of the message are both extremely predictable. It is only in the event of a problem that the language leaps up several notches in terms of complexity, as this example demonstrates:

> Pilot: I've got an emergency. Short on fuel and I'm steering to the beacon on 112.3, and I've been told to tune on to the IFR to get me to an airfield. I have less than 15 minutes fuel supply, sir.

Compare this with the following account, in which an air stewardess who attempted to break up a brawl on a flight, adds both temporal/spatial and hypothetical distance to her account:

> I was terrified ... The threat was that they were going to get that black gentleman and, if I was not there, they would have gone over and a fight would have broken out. I was worried if the windows would be kicked out, the aircraft damaged, and if we had had a fight, we had not got the facilities to stop it and there might be injuries to the passengers and other crew members.
>
> **London Evening Standard**

There's so much grammar in this text that it overflows!

4 'Annie, Sunday then. See you there. Tell Jack. Tom.'

This started life as a written message – possibly an e-mail. On its own, its meaning is difficult to unpack: where, for example, is *there*? Tell Jack what? Clearly, the message is part of a sequence of messages – the *then* in *Sunday then* (meaning *in that case*) suggests some kind of reference to Annie's previous message. Shared knowledge between reader and writer is high. Moreover, no time is lost in formalities (such as *Dear Annie... please be so kind as to tell Jack...* etc), suggesting that writer and reader share the same social space – they are familiar, if not family. In other words, there is no social distance. This suggests another role for grammar. Compare, for example, this e-mail message I received while writing this book:

> Dear Professor Thornbury,
>
> My name is Naraporn Chan-Ocha from Bangkok, Thailand. I'm a committee member of IATEFL and have been asked to liaise with the plenary speakers at IATEFL Dublin. At the conference, I'll make sure somebody accompanies you to your plenary session. We will also arrange for some participants to have lunch with you at the Burlington Hotel in the Waterloo on Thursday 30 March. Please let us know if there's anything we can do to help.
>
> Sincerely yours,
>
> Naraporn Chan-Ocha

Notice how grammaticized this text is – a count of the verb phrases alone suggests there is a lot more 'grammar' in this text than in the breakfast conversation on page 3. Look at this sentence for example (the verb phrases are underlined): *Please <u>let</u> us <u>know</u> if there<u>'s</u> anything we <u>can do</u> to <u>help</u>.* We can therefore draw another rule-of-thumb: the greater the social gap, the greater the need for grammar. (Note that a 'social gap' is not necessarily one of 'rank', but also one of familiarity.)

The highly elliptic (ie reduced) nature of talk among friends is used for stylistic effect in this advert.

'I'm off,' she said.	'Fraid so,' she said.
'Don't go,' I said.	'Thought so,' I said.
'I must,' she said.	'Guess who?' she said.
'Where to?' I said.	'Don't say,' I said.
'Not far,' she said.	'I must,' she said.
'Let's talk,' I said.	'OK,' I said.
'No time,' she said.	'Your friend,' she said.
'Someone else?' I said.	'My Vauxhall Astra!' I said.

Discovery activity

Here are some alternative ways of expressing a common function: making a request. Put them in order of grammatical complexity. Does this order reflect their degree of politeness?

Do you think you could open the door?
Open the door.

Would you mind opening the door?

I wonder if you would be so kind as to open the door?

Can you open the door?

The door!

Commentary ■ ■ ■

Most teachers I have done this task with agree that there is a fairly close correlation between degree of grammatical complexity and politeness – although perhaps *formality* would be a better expression, especially since this captures the *formal* complexity of the language. As some teachers have pointed out, non-verbal factors, such as gesture, voice-setting and intonation can make a huge difference in terms of whether the message is read as being polite or downright rude. As can the choice of vocabulary (compare: *I wonder if you would be so kind as to open the frigging door?*). Moreover, stylistic choices are very fluid and resist tight categorizations. ■

Nevertheless, it is probably fair to say that in general social distance is signalled by the use of so-called remote forms – such as the past tense (*I was wondering if you could …*) . This is especially the case in English, which does not have a distinction between *you* (formal) and *you* (familiar), such as the French *tu/vous* or the German *du/Sie*. This raises the question: given that in most classrooms – especially in adult EFL and ESL classrooms – there is not a great deal of social gap, and therefore little need to use highly elaborated polite language, what kind of activities might provide practice of 'social distance grammar'? Presumably the same question faces the teacher of French, when it comes to practising *vous* or the German teacher wishing to practise *Sie* forms. There would seem to be a strong case for role playing, ie setting up situations in the class in which the use of such forms would be required.

Grammar and distance

We have looked at four examples of de-grammared language: it's time to make some general observations. We have established a relation between grammar and social distance and expressed it in the form of a rule-of-thumb: the greater the social gap, the greater the need for grammar. Now, remember rule-of-thumb number 1? The bigger the knowledge gap, the more grammar. (Remember *Scalpel!* versus *Can you bring me that little sharp knife-like thing I use for doing appendectomies and which I left on the mantelpiece…* etc.) It is only a short step to collapse the two rules-of-thumb into a mega-rule – something like 'The greater the gap, the more the grammar'. The relation can be represented something like this:

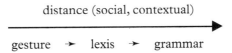

distance (social, contextual)

gesture → lexis → grammar

Moreover, the movement from lexis to grammar is not simply a case of replacing one system with another one. It is more a case of mapping grammar on to words – a process that has been called *grammaticization*.

Grammaticization

Take the case of the passive. In the absence of context information, a basic proposition such as

bite man dog

is ambiguous: does it mean the man bit the dog, or the dog bit the man? Of course, common sense suggests the latter: dogs bite men more than the other way round. Word order (or syntax) helps resolve the ambiguity:

dog bite man

Subjects of sentences typically take the first slot in the sentence (in most languages) and the subject is normally the agent (the *do-er*). Objects, on the other hand, come later in the order of things. The object is the goal of the verbal process (the *done-to*). Even without all the grammar in place, there is a natural tendency to interpret this as 'The dog bit (or bites) the man'.

But word order is not always reliable. What about:

The dog was bitten by a man.

Now the basic proposition is fully grammaticized, and the subject is no longer the agent of the action. Grammatical processes have converted the basic proposition 'dog bite man' into a passive construction in which the man, not the dog, is the agent. But why should we want to do this? What is wrong with simply saying 'A man bit the dog?'

Well, consider these two invented stories. Which would be the most appropriate middle of the story, a) or b)?

1 The dog and the cat had a disastrous day.
   a)   A man bit the dog.
   b)   The dog was bitten by a man.
   And the cat fell down a well.

2 Drug-crazed hooligans broke into my flat yesterday.
   a)   A man bit the dog.
   b)   The dog was bitten by a man.
   And someone set fire to the curtains.

Far-fetched as these contexts might appear, it should be clear that the choice of the passive is not arbitrary, but that it is a choice influenced by the speaker's idea of who or what is the topic. In (1) the dog and the cat are the topics of the story, and it is more logical, therefore, to given them the topic position (ie subject position) in the sentence, hence 'The dog was bitten by a man'. In (2), however, the dog is incidental to the story, whose topic is the drug-crazed hooligans, hence 'A man bit the dog'. You can perhaps see the relation between topicalization and passive more clearly in a real example:

A 44-year-old Lincolnshire man was cut free from his car after it had plunged down a steep embankment into trees after a collision with a lorry.

The accident happened at 8.35am yesterday on the A15 northbound carriageway at Barton, one mile from the Humber Bridge.

Rush hour traffic ground to a halt causing severe delays, after a Suzuki Jeep was in collision with a heavy goods vehicle and trailer.

The driver of the car was trapped by his legs for 20 minutes until Humberside Fire Brigade freed him.

➤ He was taken to Hull Royal Infirmary by ambulance.

After being treated for concussion and minor head and facial injuries, he was detained in hospital for observation.

The Grimsby Evening Telegraph

Notice that the sentence marked by an arrow puts the man, not the ambulance, in topic position, although it was the ambulance that 'performed' the action. But the ambulance is only incidental to the story which, right from the start, focuses on the man.

Turning a sequence of words into the passive, then, involves grammaticizing these words – a process for which we need a verb 'to grammar', since it is not so much a case of adding a 'thing' as performing a kind of operation on these words – *grammaring*, in short.

The passive is a good example of how words get grammared, but it is not the only one. Grammaring involves tagging words not only for agency (ie passivization), but for such concepts as

- number – eg by the use of plural endings: *dog – dogs*
- time – by means of tense distinctions such as *she phones, she phoned*
- aspect – that is, whether an action is viewed as being somehow extended or repeated (*she phoned* versus *she was phoning*, for example), or whether it is connected to the moment of utterance or detached from it (*she has phoned* versus *she phoned*).

What's more, grammaring can

- make statements into questions
- negate statements
- nuance a statement according to the speaker's commitment to its likelihood (*she will phone* versus *she may phone*)
- mark relations of classification versus relations of possession (*the dog food* versus *the dog's food*), classification versus identification (*a policeman* versus *the policeman*) and mass versus unit (*egg* versus *an egg*)

and a whole host of other shades of meaning. Without grammar, conveying these subtleties would require considerable lexical ingenuity.

Discovery activity

Take a basic set of propositions: how many ways can you 'grammar' them?

PRINCESS   KISS   FROG

Commentary ■ ■ ■

Here are some possible realizations of that set of propositions:

The princess kisses the frog.

The princess was kissing the frog.

A princess and a frog kissed.

Has the princess been kissed by a frog?

A princess had been kissing a frog.

Princesses will have been kissed by frogs.

Princesses and frogs may have been kissing.

It was a princess who was kissed by the frog.

What the frog did was kiss the princess.

Princess, kiss the frog!

and so on.

Try again with a slightly more complicated set:

WIZARD   DRAGON   PRINCE   OFFER ■

Discovery activity

Here is a text that has been de-grammared. That is, many of the words and endings that encode grammatical meaning have been stripped away, leaving the basic nouns, verbs and adjectives. What kind of meanings have been lost, and what kinds of ambiguity result?

50 person – injure – circus elephant – monkey – attack – gang – extortionist — beat up – master

extortionist – demand 15,000 taka ($400 U.S.) – owner – start – beat – refuse

elephant – monkey – jump – rescue – injure – serious – one – gang leader – onlooker – hurt – flee – panic

Commentary ■ ■ ■

Here is the original text:

> At least 50 persons were injured when a circus elephant and several monkeys attacked a gang of extortionists who were beating up their master... The extortionists demanded 15,000 taka ($400 U.S.) from the owner and started beating him when he refused. The elephants and monkeys jumped to the rescue, injuring seriously one of the gang leaders, while onlookers were hurt when they fled in panic.
>
> The Times of India

You may have found the 'story' quite difficult to reconstruct. Despite having a fairly clear idea of the different 'characters' involved, the relationships between them are blurred when you take away the grammar. Moreover the sequence of events is obscure, and this is not helped by the fact that the story does not fit into any commonly occurring narrative frame.■

If grammaring is a process of 'adding grammar' to propositions that are expressed lexically, what kind of activities might provide useful practice for this skill? One idea is simply to provide learners with the words and ask them to add the grammar – an activity type that used to be quite standard but has largely disappeared from ELT materials. There is an example on the next page[4].

Here is another activity that involves turning words into grammar, suggested by Adrian Underhill. It uses pictures and the Silent Way approach. Put a picture on the board and invite students to identify vocabulary they know and to write it on the board around the picture. Add, teach, correct new vocabulary as you go, if desired. Then ask students to make any sentence joining any two words in a way that remains true to what can be seen in the picture. Correct and practise as required. Join some to make extended sentences.

8. An Odd Revenge

every evening
from seven o'clock till
   midnight
the music lover
to sit
leaning back
   comfortably
the armchair
to listen
to be fond of
the radio set
to switch on
to increase the volume
to make too much noise
to think only of oneself
selfish
the neighbour
the flat
next door

the thin wall
separated by
to wish to work
not to be able to
   concentrate
the study
the writing table
foolish
to try hard
to find
impossible
to be at one's wit's end
unable
because of
one Tuesday evening
he cannot stand it any
   longer

to take one's revenge
to get one's own back
to leave
in a rage
the radio shop
to buy
the most powerful
to drown
to blare
neither of the two
to stop up one's ears
the result
unexpected
not to hear anything
   at all
to fail
ridiculous

Summary

In this chapter I used the following as examples of language that was primarily lexical and only minimally grammaticized:
1 NO PARKING
2 THREE SHARE LOTTERY FORTUNE
3 'Tickets, please.'
4 'Annie, Sunday then. See you there. Tell Jack. Tom.'

I put the case that the 'de-caffeinated' nature of these texts is possible only because the writer/speaker and reader/listener share a great deal of common knowledge. This shared knowledge makes the fine-tuning associated with grammatical meaning fairly redundant. Knowledge is shared if it can be retrieved from the immediate context (both in space and in time), or if it can be retrieved by reference to common experience. (*Tickets, please* is what you'd expect a ticket collector to say.) On the other hand, grammar is enlisted wherever there is a distance to overcome – either in context, knowledge, or in social relations. This suggests a basic rule: the greater the distance, the more the need for grammar.

In the next chapter we will see how this *grammar = distance* formula relates to the way grammar is acquired, in both first and second language acquisition. This view of grammar as a process – something we *do* linguistically, when faced by distance – is known as grammaticizing, a rather clumsy word that was invented to make up for the fact that, in English, there is no verb *to grammar*. So, how is it we learn to grammar?

References

1 *Active Study Dictionary*. Harlow: Longman
2 These headlines were taken from Cooper, G. 1987 *Red Tape Holds Up New Bridge*. New York: Perigee Books
3 Mell, J. 'Emergency calls – Messages out of the blue.' In *Le Transpondeur,* no. 11, December 1993, pp84-6
4 Fleming, G. and Fougasse 1961 *Guided Composition for Students of English*. London: University of London Press

Chapter 2   **Learning to grammar**

In the last chapter we looked at language whose effectiveness relies largely on words alone, the rest of the communicative work being done by inferencing – from the context, from shared knowledge, or through familiarity with our speaking or writing partners. Lexical communication is also a characteristic of early learner speech, whether in first or second language learning, as these examples demonstrate:

- 'All gone milk!'
- 'Me Tarzan. You Jane.'

In this chapter we continue our investigation of grammarless language by looking at learner language. Again, the intention is to find out what grammar *adds* by looking at language where it is absent.

First language grammaring: *All gone milk!*

Early child language, as in *All gone milk*, is low on grammar. Initially communicating solely through gesture and tone of voice, children start to produce their first words at around twelve months. These are individual words that serve to refer to, or describe, features of their everyday world: *ball*, *cat*, *dirty*, *Daddy*, *shoe*. They also use language to get things done – *Give!*, *Put!*, *Up!*, *Stop!* – and to communicate social meanings: *Hi*, *Bye-bye*. These two major language functions – sometimes called, respectively, the *referential* and the *interpersonal* – form a kind of template for all subsequent language use. And (as we saw in Chapter 1) even adults still express these functions purely lexically at times:

Pedestrian *(to companion, nodding towards a car that happens to be passing)*:　　Rolls.
Parent *(to child who is obstructing the footpath)*:　　Mind!

At around 18 months children typically move from a one-word stage to a two or more word stage. Here is a conversation between a 15-month-old child and his mother[1]:

Timmy:　Car.
Mother:　Nice car!
Timmy:　Go.
Mother:　Where's it going?

Compare this with a similar conversation eight months later:

Timmy:　Car go.
Mother:　It's going very fast.

Notice that what once took two 'turns' to express is now compressed into one: *Car go*. Timmy has moved from words only to mini-sentences. Mini-sentences, note, not simply two words arbitrarily strung together. These mini-sentences are not entirely ungrammaticized. Certain kinds of relationship seem to be encoded in the word order, even if the words themselves are not inflected. Thus agent + process relationships are expressed as a basic subject-verb framework (*Car go*). *Teddy eat*, even to a child, means something different from *eat teddy*. This contrasts with the 'sentences' produced by a chimpanzee (called Nim) that was taught to use sign language[2]:

banana Nim banana Nim
banana me Nim me
banana eat me Nim
Nim eat Nim eat
banana me eat banana

The chimpanzee seems to be able to produce a limited set of randomly ordered sentences, including a lot of repetition, on a limited number of topics. It is more like list making than sentence production. A child, however, even at the two-word utterance stage, can produce a greater variety of sentence patterns, expressing a relatively wide range of meanings:

- agent + action   (*daddy kick*)
- action + affected (*throw stick*)
- possessor + possession (*daddy coat*)
- nomination (*that ball*)
- recurrence (*more ball*)
- negation (*no ball*)

The fact that these are not one-offs is demonstrated by the systematic adaptation of these patterns, eg:

that ball

that doll

that daddy

that boy

etc.

From the age of two children are producing longer utterances, but they are still relatively ungrammaticized: *Clare have banana; letter fall out mummy book; dada get knife take skin off apple*[3].

Meanwhile, as well as the stringing together of words into increasingly longer sequences, a parallel process is taking place. Children often take on board already 'prefabricated' chunks – that is, a phrase or expression that is learned and used as if it were a single unit – a case of 'learning the tune before the words'. The chunk may take the form of a sentence starter, like *gimme...* (for *give me*) or a social formula, like *See you later!* These chunks typically display a grammatical complexity beyond the child's current generative capacity. They are used appropriately, but without any understanding of their internal structure. For example[4]:

(Child is putting coat on the wrong way)
Mother: That's upside down.
Child: No, I want to upside down.

Researchers suggest that many of these chunks are 'stored' for later analysis into their components. Thus *gimme* is segmented into *give me* which is then able to generate *give Mummy, give her, give him,* etc. Formulaic learning of this kind may provide the raw material for grammaring. (Of course, the formulae can be misanalysed: my younger sister wrongly analysed the formulaic response to a sneeze – *God bless you!* – as *Scott splash you!*)

At about three, a major advance occurs, as sentences increase in grammatical complexity:

Child: Daddy have breaked the spade all up and – and – and – it broken – and – he did hurt his hand on it and – and – and – it's gone all sore and...

Notice that the basic lexical propositions (*Daddy break spade, spade broken, Daddy hurt hand, hand gone sore*) have been grammaticized through the use of auxiliary verbs (*have, did, 's*), verb inflexions (*breaked*) and pronouns referring back to previously mentioned propositions (*it, he, his*). And the whole is sewn together by the co-ordinating conjunction *and.* While still departing from adult language norms, there is a major leap from lexicalized to grammaticized language.

But even at this stage children still have trouble interpreting such relatively subtle grammatical distinctions as, for example, the difference between active and passive constructions. They still tend to operate on the basis of a simple word-order grammar, hearing *Action Man was rescued by Lady Penelope* as *Action Man rescued Lady Penelope*.

Mother tongue acquisition, then, follows a progression from lexical to grammatical processes. Acquiring your first language (L1) is, to a large extent, a process of learning to grammar. We can represent it like this:

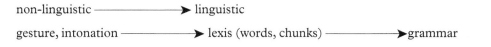

non-linguistic ⎯⎯⎯⎯⎯⟶ linguistic

gesture, intonation ⎯⎯⎯⟶ lexis (words, chunks) ⎯⎯⎯⟶grammar

Discovery activity

Here are some examples of language that a child, Adam, produced over a period of time. The researcher, Peccei[1], has divided them into three different stages. Can you detect a grammaring process over the three stages? What kind of 'rule' does Adam seem to be operating at each stage?

Stage 1	**Stage 2**	**Stage 3**
Adam home.	I like drink it.	That what I do.
Adam go hill.	I Adam driving.	Can I put them on?
Like Adam book shelf.	I making coffee.	You want me?
Pick Adam up.	Wake me up.	You watch me.
	Why hitting me?	
	What me doing?	
	Why me spilled it?	

Commentary ■ ■ ■

What the researcher found interesting in the examples above was the development of the child's pronoun system, specifically the differentiation between *I* and *me*. Note that at Stage 1 Adam uses a lexical device to identify himself: his own name. At Stage 2 he uses pronouns but he seems to be operating on a simple word-order rule: at the beginning of the sentence use *I*; at any other place use *me*. This is not a bad rule-of-thumb, since *I* does start sentences as often as not. But it is not until Stage 3 that he seems to have internalized the much more abstract grammatical rule: use *I* for subject and *me* for object, irrespective of position in sentence. ■

Second language grammaring: *Me Tarzan, you Jane*

As with first language acquisition, a similar lexical-to-grammatical direction seems to be the case for second language acquisition. (The main difference is that most second language learners do not go so far along the road.) Early second language productions are mainly lexical. If there is any grammar it seems rather hit-and-miss. Here, for example, is an elementary Spanish learner of English describing Christmas:

> *The best day in my life is one when my family is together, because celebrate the christmas day. My brothers and your wife living out Barcelona, my sister and your husband lived in Barcelona, so do I. Every body go to parents house. Eaten two o'clock, we eat turkey.*

I said that the fledgling grammar *seems* hit-and-miss, but, as with children, learners seem to be operating on some rudimentary rules-of-thumb. One researcher, for example, found that learners pass through a stage when they tend to attach the ending *-ing* to action verbs, irrespective of tense. They seem to be using *-ing* simply to mark the presence of a verb: *I going work by bus; I eating everyday Burger King*, etc. Clumsy as this may seem, it marks an important step from using purely lexical means to using more grammatical ones. At first the *-ing* ending is applied indiscriminately to all verbs. But over time, the learners in the study started to restrict the use of *-ing* to certain contexts, and mainly as a marker of 'pastness': *Yesterday I no working*. Other favoured contexts for *-ing* were in subordinate clauses (*He the man who I talking him*) and verbal complements, ie constructions where one verb follows another, eg *I want working* and *I can doing any job*.

Why *-ing*? The researcher hypothesized that, of all the possible word endings in English, *-ing* is the most easily identified: it is a whole syllable and it is phonetically simple and regular. As grammaring processes start to emerge, *-ing* is a convenient tool for flagging 'verbiness', or, more specifically, 'action'. At first, all verbs are flagged. Then the learner starts to discriminate between varying degrees of distance: present and past. The later use of *-ing* in the more relatively specialised contexts of pastness, subordinate clauses and verbal complements suggests learners are aware of the more grammaticized nature of these contexts and need to flag them accordingly. Not yet aware of how these specialized meanings are signalled, they use the all purpose *-ing*, as if to say 'here be grammar'.

Discovery activity

Here is another piece of elementary level writing. Notice the learner's use of the *-ing* form. What kind of principles does he or she seem to be operating on?

> *The sunday night past, the doorbell rangs, I opened the door and I has got a big surprise, my brother was stoping in the door. He was changing a lot of, but he was having the same smile as always. He was more tall and more thin. He was having many hear but him looking was very interesting, my brother always was a goodlooking. [...] We speaked all night and we remembered a lot of thinks.*

Commentary ■ ■ ■

There seem to be two principles at work here: one is the use of *-ing* to mark what are called stative verbs – verbs that describe a state rather than an activity: *was stoping* (for *standing*), *was changing*, *was having*, and the other principle is to overgeneralize the ending to make nouns – on the principle of *smoke/smoking*, *swim/swimming* perhaps. Thus: *him looking* (for *his appearance*) and *a goodlooking*. The same principle may be behind the derivation of such established Spanish coinages as *footing* (for *running*), *camping* (for *campsite*) and *lifting* (for *face-lift*). ■

In another study, by Perdue and Klein (1992)[5], the language development of two Italian men living (but not studying) in London was compared over time. Whereas one of the learners, Andrea, seemed to make steady progress in terms of grammaticizing, the other, Santo, seemed to be stuck in a lexical backwater. Here were some of things the researchers noted.

Initially, both learners sometimes used a non-standard verb–subject sentence pattern, as in *come back the brigade fire*. Over time, Andrea stopped using this construction, but Santo retained it, using it frequently. As in the '-ing study' mentioned above, Andrea began to develop a distinction between the base form of the verb (eg *do*) and the verb + *-ing* (eg *doing*), using the former for the main events of a narrative and the latter for background actions, following the principle, perhaps, of 'the more distance, the more grammar'. He also learned to distinguish between base forms and past simple forms, in both regular (eg *finished*) and irregular verbs (eg *found*). Santo made no such systematic verb ending distinctions and only learned a handful of irregular past tense verbs, but never used a form like *finished*. Other areas in which Andrea made progress but Santo didn't were in the use of pronouns and in the forming of subordinate clauses.

In accounting for the different rates of progress, the researchers suggest that Andrea had a stronger desire not to be considered a foreigner. In other words, he was motivated by the wish to integrate into the target language community. Santo, on the other hand, seemed not to care a lot about integration and was happy enough to speak a pidginized form of English, so long as he succeeded in getting his meanings across. It may also have been the case that Andrea did *not* feel he was getting his meanings across, and needed to fine-tune his output accordingly. We will return to the question of motivation again in Chapter 5.

>> pp73–6

Discovery activity

We saw that, in first language learning, the acquisition of pronoun rules (eg for *I* and *me*) occurs over stages. The same seems to be true for second language pronoun acquisition, although the stages are slightly different.

Here are some typical pronoun errors in the order in which they commonly persist, ie those at the end of the list persist longer than those at the beginning. Can you account for this order using the principle of 'the more distance, the more grammar'?

1 the man take camera and the man running... (for *he runs*)
2 Me Tarzan ... (for *I am Tarzan*)
3 My sister and your husband... (for *her husband*)
4 ... and his children (for *their children*)
5 ... and the man running and she drop a camera... (for *he drops*)

Commentary ■ ■ ■

The first stage (1) is the pre-grammatical one where pronouns are not used at all – either nouns are repeated, or the slot is left empty (eg *Kicking* for *He is kicking*). This is the purely lexical stage.

Stage 2 marks the beginning of pronoun use, typically to refer to the speaker, and *I* and *me* are often used interchangeably. The successive stages (3 to 5) mark increasing degrees of distance. At stage 3 the learner makes a two-way distinction between self and not-self, typically using *I/me* for the former, and *you* (or *your*) for both second and third person, ie non-self. The next distinction to be made is between singular and plural (stage 4), and finally, between male and female (stage 5). Interestingly, the gender distinction is the last acquired, suggesting that – psychologically, at least – gender is a more 'distant' concept than either person or number. ■

In commenting on the acquisition order of pronouns, Johnston (1987)[6] notes:

> Learners do not acquire pronouns as if they were arranged in a single ensemble or list, since some features are preconditions for others, and must precede them in acquisition. If we wish to visualize the process, it might be convenient to think of it as the growth of a tree; twigs cannot grow before branches... Unfortunately, this state of affairs is not often taken into account by teachers or textbooks, and learners tend to be presented with whole sets of pronouns in a single lesson. The result is, very predictably, confusion and frustration.

We will come back to metaphors of growth and emergence in Chapter 4. Meanwhile, it is worth emphasizing the point that, however much learners may want to start with a fully operational grammatical system, there is a long stage where the best they can do is simply cobble individual words together in the fashion of *Me Tarzan, you Jane* or *Mistah Kurtz: he dead*. Moreover, this largely lexical stage is likely to be prolonged when the need to communicate takes precedence over linguistic complexity. Classroom talk, for example, is often reduced to a kind of pidgin, as in this exchange, from Nunan 1991[7], where real communication is taking place, but at a level that is almost purely lexical:

T	In Australia, er, bicycle, er, we wear a helmet.	**T**	Motorbike.
S	Helmet.	**S**	Yes, yes. Bicycle, no. China, bicycle no. Motor, yes.
Ss	Yes, yes.	**T**	Ah huh!
T	Special helmet.	**S**	Cap, cap.
Ss	Ohh.	**S**	Cap.
S	Malaysia, same, same.	**S**	Hat on, hat, hat.
T	Same in Malaysia?	**T**	Hat.
Ss	Yes, yes.	**Ss**	Hat. Hat.
S	Moto, moto.	**T**	Ah, in Australia, motor bike, yes. Yes, yes, yes. Bicycle, yes, good. Children special helmet. Helmet, mm, special helmet.
T	In China, a little or a lot		

There is good reason to believe that communication at this grammatically reduced level may be counter-productive. Yet this is often the kind of language that emerges in unmonitored 'free speaking'. After all, it is difficult – in the cut-and-thrust of real communication – to allocate attention both to the medium and the message.

A diet of nothing else but unrehearsed fluency activities, such as group discussions or communicative games, may make learners over-reliant on lexical processes at the expense of developing their grammatical competence. Such learners – that is, those who get stuck at a mainly lexical level of processing – are said to have *fossilized*. Here is a description[8] of a learner who has come to rely almost entirely on de-grammared language:

> Sachiko-san was as unabashed and unruly in her embrace of English as most of her compatriots were reticent and shy. ... She was happy to plunge ahead without a second thought for grammar, scattering meanings and ambiguities as she went. Plurals were made singular, articles were dropped, verbs were rarely inflected, and word order was exploded – often, in fact, she seemed to be making Japanese sentences with a few English words thrown in. Often, moreover, to vex the misunderstandings further, she spoke both languages at once...

To summarize, we can propose a simple rule-of-thumb:

> *The greater the processing demands, the more reliance on a lexical system. The fewer demands, the more chance of grammaring.*

« pp7–9 Notice that this rule sits uncomfortably with the 'first law of grammar' discussed in Chapter 1, ie that the greater the distance, the more grammar. Herein lies a basic dilemma for language learners and their teachers: the need for speed discourages grammaring, while the demands of distance require it. Thus, there is a constant trade-off between speed and complexity, such that learners tend to fall into two groups – fast but lexical and slow but grammatical. The fast and lexical learner can make rapid headway early on, but, as in the case of the Hare and the Tortoise, it is the plodder who probably wins the race, even though he risks losing many conversational partners along the way.

Grammar up!

What does this mean in terms of classroom teaching? Certainly not that fluency activities should be abandoned. Fluency activities are necessary in order to help make language production fluid and automatic. But they need to be balanced with other activities that encourage learners to develop their grammaring skills – that is, to increase the complexity, not just the automaticity, of their developing language system. Learners need to be reminded that an over reliance on words alone may stunt their linguistic growth: they need to be told, from time to time, to *Grammar up!*

Activities directed at this end would need to take account of the two rules of thumb we have established:

1 The greater the distance, the more the grammar. (That is to say, where there is a knowledge gap or a social gap, words alone will be insufficient to bridge that gap.)
2 The fewer processing demands, the more the grammar. (That is to say, where there is reduced pressure and more planning time, there is a greater likelihood of 'grammaring' as opposed to 'wording'.)

In other words, activities designed to promote grammaring will need to reduce the learner's dependence on the immediate context and on words alone and to provide an incentive to enlist grammar in order to make meanings crystal clear. At the same time, activities will need to provide learners with the right conditions – including sufficient processing time – so that they can marshal their grammaring skills. Finally, they will need clear messages as to how precise they have been: feedback must be explicit and immediate. We can represent these factors as:

Grammaring activities

- low context dependence
- high incentive for precision
- low pressure
- high feedback

What kinds of activities would meet one or more of these conditions? Let's start with the 'low context' condition. We have already seen that grammar is a function of distance –

depriving learners of useful contextual information increases the distance, and therefore, in theory at least, increases the need for grammar. Compare these two tasks:

1 In pairs, look at the sequence of pictures and then take turns to describe it to each other.

2 Look at this sequence of pictures. Keep it hidden from your partner. Describe the sequence to your partner.

In the first task, where both students can see the pictures, there is no context gap to bridge. Students in this situation often get away with relying on lexis, pointing and fairly reduced grammar – unless the teacher is eavesdropping! In the second task, however, in order for the listener to get the gist of the story, the speaker will have to use more than simply words and gestures.

The problem is, though, that as the task stands there is little or no *incentive* for the listener to listen for the gist. We need a motive:

3 You have seen an incident in the street. Describe the incident to your partner. (Keep the picture hidden!) Your partner has to decide who should be arrested and who should be rewarded.

Now we have a motive. To achieve the task outcome the listener is going to have to attend carefully and even ask questions in order to clarify details. The listener's understanding of the story acts as a form of feedback to the speaker. But we are placing a very high processing load on the speaker. It is a lot to ask of students to tell the story, grammaticize it sufficiently and deal with unexpected questions. With the best will in the world, they may still go to pieces, grammatically speaking.

One way round this is to simply provide the *words* the student needs, and leave the grammaring up to them:

couple	*chase*	*pickpocket*	*thief*
shopping	*old woman*	*follow*	*thank*
carrier bag	*karate chop*	*steal*	*reward*
handbag	*catch*	*purse*	*run off*

Another way is to allow the speakers to prepare their story in advance – making notes, if necessary, and even consulting a grammar book or the teacher. Meanwhile, to keep them busy, their partners can be preparing a story of their own: we now need two stories (or two versions of the same story), which suggests a further modification. Give one student the set of pictures on the previous page and give their partner the set of pictures below.

4 You and your partner have both seen an incident in the street. Describe the incident you have seen to your neighbour using these pictures. (There are some words to help you.) Then listen to your partner's story. You have to decide if you both saw the same incident, or a completely different incident.

Here is part of a transcript of two students doing this task. Note the way the grammar is made more complex as the meaning is negotiated, particularly in the underlined parts:

S1 ...When a young couple of people go straight ahead on the street they are surprisingly advised that one young girl going behind them are taking a purse into the back of the young woman.

S2 Excuse me, you say that they are advising?

S1 Yes.

S2 Who are advise him?

S1 A man who are standing up on the... in one... in one... shop... in front of one shop.

S2 In the left side?

S1 Yes, in the left side from the young couple. Yes. He advised this young couple and the lady... the young lady shout the police: 'Police, police, this young girl going... running... it's a thief' and the police go back to the young woman. In this moment an old woman are crossing near the thief who was running opposite to her and <u>the old woman beat, no hit, the young thief</u> and and...

S2 In the picture <u>you can see as the old woman</u> (**S1:** Yes) <u>hit the young thief?</u>

S1 Yes, <u>I can</u> (**S2:** I can't) <u>see the old woman who hit the young thief.</u>

S2 So our pictures are different because I...

S1 Yes, I think so, because the policeman doesn't do anything in my picture, in my history.

S2 In my fourth picture a police catch the thiefs.

S1 Oh, it's a very efficient police... policeman.

S2 But <u>I don't see er nothing about er an old woman hitting the young thief.</u>

Discovery activity

Here is a simple task: *Tell your partner how you spent your weekend.*

How could you build into it the task features that are conducive to grammaring, ie low context, high incentive, low pressure, high feedback?

Commentary ■ ■ ■

Note there is already an element of distance in this task, since there is a natural context gap: we are talking about the past, and a past that was not shared. Compare this with a task such as 'Tell your partner what other students in the classroom are doing right now'.

However, providing an incentive for students to take the communication seriously enough to want to grammar it up is a challenge. One way is to build into it some kind of game-type element, for example: 'Tell your partner how you spent your weekend. Include at least one total lie. See if they can guess what it is.' Or: 'Tell your partner how you *didn't* spend your weekend. They then tell you what they think you really did.' ■

One way of both providing a distancing effect and removing some of the pressure is to ask students to *write*. Writing, by its nature, requires more thought. Not only that, it exists in time, unlike speech, which, unless you record it, is elusive. Anything written, therefore, is available for review and correction. But writing is time-consuming and, ultimately, may encourage too much concern for getting things right. Communication will slow to a crawl. Is there a way of injecting a bit of the urgency of naturally occurring speech into writing?

Conversations in 'slow motion'

Computer-mediated communication has provided an answer in the form of live *chat*. Chat programmes allow people to communicate across distances by sending and receiving short written messages to each other in real time. Because the communication is both informal and immediate, but slightly delayed by the demands of writing, it has been called 'conversation in slow motion'. Nevertheless, this slowing down frees just a little bit more attention to focus on the form of the message as much as on its content. The combination of distance (ie context gap) and processing time makes it a potentially rich site for grammaring.

On the following page there is an example of computer-mediated chat: this takes place between two students of English in Spain (sharing a keyboard) and a student in France. They are using software which allows them to choose from a menu of characters and backgrounds. But the words are entirely their own.

There is a way of simulating computer chat in the classroom, and that is simply by asking students to have 'paper conversations' with each other. They pass a sheet of paper backwards and forwards and 'talk'. Here, for example, is the beginning of a role play in which one student asks his 'mother' permission to get a tattoo.

S1 Mum, I want to ask you something.

S2 What is the question?

S1 I want to get a tattoo.

S2 You can do what you want.

S1 OK.

S2 OK what?

S1 I'm going to get a tattoo.

S2 With one condicion, but it has to say 'I love mum'.

S1 Are you crazy?

Another example of the way writing can promote grammaring is through activity summaries. I often wrap up a class or group chat by asking students in groups to write a summary of what has been said for a student who happens to be absent that day (there's always one!). This is what one group wrote:

> *We talked about our life inside the house. All three do the dishes and only Pilar doesn't do the ironing. Silvia and me are a little untidy but Pilar said that she is very tidy and everytime puts the things away. Otherwise, Silvia and me make the bed every morning, and Pilar doesn't make it because she don't have time (in the morning).*
>
> *Silvia and Pilar have problems with the people who shares their flats because they spend a lot of time in the bath, but I don't have this problem. Silvia and me loves making cakes. Pilar also likes cooking but her job makes that she don't have time for cook.*

Task repetition

Another technique that facilitates grammaring is task repetition. Simply getting the learners to repeat the task, with different partners, or in the next lesson, is a way of producing more grammatically complex language. Having done the activity once – as a kind of rehearsal – learners now have more spare attention to devote to the form of their output. Repetition serves to lower the pressure, increasing the likelihood of grammaring.

For example, take the task we looked at earlier: *Tell your partner how you spent your weekend.*

One way of building repetition into this task is to have them tell as many people in the class as possible, with a view to finding out whose weekend was the most similar / most different to theirs. Another is through the 4-3-2 technique. This involves learners performing the same task but within successively decreasing time limits. For example, Student A talks about a topic or tells a story in four minutes, while his or her partner listens and keeps an eye on the clock. Student B then does the same. Then Student A retells his or her piece, but this time in three minutes, and so on. The repetition of the task encourages greater linguistic complexity, while the decreasing time limit is aimed at promoting greater fluency.

Discovery activity

In order to study the effects of task repetition, Martin Bygate[9] showed a learner a short extract of a cartoon film and asked her to retell the story. Two days later, without warning or any intervening preparation, the task was repeated. Here are the transcripts of the task. What improvements do you notice?

T1: First attempt

I saw a little film about a cat and a mouse and the cat would like to eat the mouse but the mouse disliked this and she escape and she run up the wall and there was a board who was covered over and over with plate and and bowls and the mouse put it down and the cat was afraid that the plates are break damaged and she tr erm catch all the things and in the end there was er a big a big I don't know a big hill with dishes and the cat stand there and try to hold the dishes to save it but the mouse smiled and she comes up over the plates and she erm played with the tail of the cat she took a bath in the cat's milk and then she took the tail of the cat as a towel and she erm took the hairs from the cat away and she gave her erm she touch her with her feet and then the landlady come and the mouse erm touch the cat with the feet and the cat couldn't hold the dishes and all the plates and the bowls break and go go down and all the things was damaged and the landlady took the cat and go to punish to give punishment to the cat and the mouse was very happy and she took erm she took a board over the door who stand er a nice house ( ) so that's all

T2: Second attempt, two days later, without warning

I saw a very nice cartoon about Tom and Jerry and er the cat tried to catch the mouse the mouse er run up to a ca... to a cupboard cupboard and there were a lot of dishes especially plates and the mouse put up the plates and taked down and the cat wun to take off the plates because he had fear that the dish will get break and the cat collected all the dishes and in the end there is a lot and um very high just like a hill and the mouse come down came down and she jump jumped on the cat's nose and then she jump in the milk from the cat and she took a bath and after that she used the tail of the cat as a towel and she took the hairs away and she kicked the cat and all the dishes falling down and all the plates are broken the house lady came and she saw this and she picked up the cat to give her a terrible punishment I think so and the mouse was smile smiled and she go to erm to a hole and she put a sign where stand stood this is a nice home my sweet home

Commentary ■ ■ ■

The researcher comments that the second attempt at the task shows a striking improvement in accuracy in terms of vocabulary, idiomaticity, grammatical markers and syntax. He added, 'There were also signs that the speaker became more fluent: at T1 she used a lot or repetition *before* producing words and phrases; at T2 she repeated rather to self-correct *after* producing words and phrases.' On the basis of this and other, more detailed, studies the researcher concludes that task repetition 'can be a powerful help for learners to integrate fluency, accuracy and complexity'. ■

One further way of building into a task a degree of distance (and, remember, distance is good for grammaring) is to formalize it. Writing, by its very nature, does this to some extent. Another way is to exploit the effect of *social* distance that occurs when students are asked to perform, eg by making a formal report of an activity to the class. After conducting a survey, for example, students in groups prepare a report which one of them delivers to the class – preferably standing up or in front of the class. Anybody who has ever had to present a report at a meeting, or to speak in public, will be aware of the pressure to 'get it right' – what one writer calls 'being on one's linguistic best behaviour'. Presenting the report to another class would up the stakes even more; so too would audio or video recording the presentation.

Here is a transcript of a student reporting on a class survey. Notice how the speaker corrects herself, showing that some of her attention is available for grammaring, and that the public performance provides an incentive to get it right.

> *Nobody has ever smoked a Cuban cigar. Everybody has ride a horse and written a poem. Everybody has found money in the street except Mario, and three people have lost their keys and three has... has not... haven't. Only Oliver and Mercè has ever... has... have visited Guggenheim Museum. Jesús has done military service but Oliver and Mario haven't done... it. Only Alejandra has fall in love with two people at the same time.*

Strange stories

Compare these two narratives:
1 A man went into a bar. He asked the barman for a drink. He took it to a table, sat down and drank it. Then he got up, paid the barman, and left the bar.
2 A man went into a bar. He asked the admiral for a hairdryer. He took it to a surfboard, rolled over and hid it. Then he lay down, punched the admiral, and left the bar.

The first narrative fulfils our expectations of what happens when people go into bars (although the sequence may differ slightly in different cultures). In other words, it matches our mental *schema* of a bar-type scenario. A schema (plural: *schemata*) is a knowledge structure stored in memory. Thus we get to our place of work and back using a stored 'map', or schema, of the route. Tourists negotiating their way round a strange town typically do not have a schema for that town so they have to consult a (real) map. Of course they may have a more generalized, cultural schema for the way towns are typically distributed (high street, cathedral square, market place, business area, etc). Schemata also often take the form of *scripts*, that is, a sequence of events in memory. The restaurant script is a much-quoted one: you go in, the waiter greets you, shows you to a table, gives you the menu, you order, etc. Compare this to a fast-food outlet script.

The second narrative above does not follow the 'bar script' – to the extent that it comes across as nonsense or surrealistic or like a dream. Because it doesn't match our expectations, it is much harder to process: there is a schema-gap, if you like. If you were telling this story in such a way that your listener was able to make sense of it, you would have to work much harder, linguistically speaking. You would have to fill in the schema gap, like this:

> A man went into a bar. He asked the admiral (who was one of the regulars) for a hairdryer (because it had been raining and he was soaked, and because the admiral kept a collection of electric appliances in a suitcase he carried around with him)... etc.

This story requires a lot more grammaring (as well as 'wording') in order to make it coherent.

Similarly, imagine we tell the first narrative again, but in reverse, starting from the man's leaving the bar, rather than his arriving there:

> A man left a bar. He had just paid the barman, having got up from where he had sat in order to have a drink, which he had previously taken to a table. Prior to that he had asked the barman for the drink, after having entered the bar.

Again, changing the perspective – even of a familiar schema – requires a greater degree of grammaring.

≪ pp10–11 Newspapers do this constantly when they report events. They seldom begin at the beginning of a story. Rather they start with what they consider its most newsworthy feature – usually the outcome, as in this story we looked at earlier. (The events are numbered in the actual order that they happened.)

> (6) A 44-year-old Lincolnshire man was cut free from his car after

> (3) it had plunged down a steep embankment into trees after a collision with a lorry.

> (1) The accident happened at 8.35am yesterday on the A15 northbound carriageway at Barton, one mile from the Humber Bridge.

> (4) Rush hour traffic ground to a halt causing severe delays after (2) a Suzuki Jeep was in collision with a heavy goods vehicle and trailer.

> (5) The driver of the car was trapped by his legs for 20 minutes until Humberside Fire Brigade freed him.

> (7) He was taken to Hull Royal Infirmary by ambulance.

> After (8) being treated for concussion and minor head and facial injuries, (9) he was detained in hospital for observation.

Discovery activity

In the newspaper text above, what grammatical as well as lexical features have been used to help the reader untangle the actual order in which things happened?

Commentary ■ ■ ■

Lexical means of signalling the order of events include sequencing conjunctions (*after... until...*). Grammatical devices include the use of tense, especially the way the past perfect (*it had plunged...*) directs the reader to an action that happened prior to the event focus.
■

The grammaring up potential of strange schemata suggests a number of classroom tasks:

- Students take a familiar scenario (eg going to a supermarket, travelling to work, etc) and make adjustments to it and then tell their partner, who has to tell it back.
- Students take a selection of unrelated pictures and weave them into a story.
- Students read an unusual story, and tell it to their group, who have to summarize it.
- Students tell a familiar story from an unfamiliar point of view, for example, 'modernizing' or 'feminizing' a traditional folk tale.
- Students take a sequence of narrative events and write a newspaper report, starting with the outcome.

Summary

We have looked at ways of grammaring up language production tasks, including:

- information gap – to increase distance by reducing shared knowledge and reliance on context
- personalization – to increase intrinsic interest and give an incentive to communicate
- game element – to provide further incentive to fine-tune
- writing – to provide a sense of distance as well as to allow processing time
- repetition – to increase processing opportunities
- performance – to increase social distance
- schema-bending – to reduce shared knowledge.

It is important to note that these grammaring activities need not be focused on any specific grammatical feature, least of all a pre-selected one. Rather, they are designed to increase the overall complexity of the learner's output and to encourage a general movement from reliance solely on lexical language to an appreciation of the usefulness of grammatical processes.

In the next chapter we will look at ways of raising learners' awareness of specific features of process grammar, especially by means of activities that manipulate the input they receive.

References

1 Peccei, J.S. 1999 *Child Language (2nd edition)*. London: Routledge
2 Terrance, H.S. 1979 *Nim: A Chimpanzee Who Learned Sign Language*. Washington Square Press, p319
3 Halliday, M. 1975 *Learning How to Mean*. London: Edward Arnold
4 Crystal, D. 1987 *The Cambridge Encyclopedia of Language*. Cambridge: Cambridge University Press, p243
5 Perdue, C. and Klein, W. 1992 'Why does the production of some learners not grammaticalize?' In *Studies in Language Acquisition, no. 14*, pp259-72
6 Johnston, M. 'Understanding Learner Language.' In Nunan, D. (ed.) 1987 *Applying Second Language Acquisition Research*. Sydney: National Curriculum Resource Centre, Adult Migrant Education Program
7 Nunan, D. 1991 *Language Teaching Methodology*. Hemel Hempstead: Prentice Hall
8 Iyer, P. 1992 *The Lady and the Monk*. London: Black Swan, p101
9 Bygate, M. 'Effects of task repetition: appraising the developing language of learners.' In Willis, J. and Willis, D. (eds.) 1996 *Challenge and Change in Language Teaching*. Oxford: Heinemann ELT and 'Task as the context for framing, reframing and unframing of language.' In *System, 27*, pp33-48

Chapter 3   Noticing grammar

In Chapters 1 and 2, we put the case for grammar being considered less as a set of facts about the language than as a kind of mental process that is activated whenever an utterance is in need of fine-tuning. This verb-like, process view of grammar seems to apply not only to the production of language, but to the way grammar develops in both first and second language acquisition. Left to their own devices, however, many second language learners do not get very far with these developmental processes – in some cases, little or no grammaring takes place at all. So, what can we do to nudge the process along? In this chapter we take a look at the kind of things that teachers can do to oil the grammaring processes.

Instruction plus and instruction minus

Me *(meeting a student of mine in downtown Cairo)*: Hey Hamdi, where are you going?
Hamdi: I go to Sporting Club.
Me *(unable to resist a chance to correct)*: Go?
Hamdi *(impatiently)*: Oh, go, going, went!

Question: How was I to interpret Hamdi's outburst?

1 'Correction is for classrooms – the street is for communication!'

2 'You understood what I meant, so why the correction?'

3 'Search me. I still don't know the difference between *go/going/went*.'

4 'Don't expect me to say what I mean and get it right at the same time!'

5 All of the above.

My interpretation is probably 5: All of the above. Hamdi was right: my correction was definitely out of order, and, it's true, I knew exactly what he was trying to say. (Contextual clues like the fact he was carrying a tennis racquet helped.) Whether or not Hamdi 'knew' the difference between *go*, *going* and *went* is less clear: you can know something in theory, but you may not be able to put it into practice. In learning a second language, as in learning to drive, there is a lag between 'know what' and 'can do'. Finally, with regard to point 4, my experience as both language learner and language teacher has taught me that it is very hard – often impossible – to focus on communication and accuracy at the same time. Or, put another way, you can't devote equal attention to meaning and form. It's a condition not unlike that of the US president of whom it was said that he couldn't walk and chew gum.

The problem is, however, that good language learners *can* walk and chew gum, metaphorically speaking. The ability to say what you mean on cue and, at the same time, to get it right is perhaps the defining characteristic of a proficient speaker. Unless this capacity is developed, there is a danger that learners like Hamdi will follow the path of least resistance and *never* get beyond the *Me Tarzan, you Jane* phase of second language development. In other words, the system settles for second best and simply shuts down. After all, *I go to Sporting Club* does the job, even if it is not technically precise. The effort involved in cranking up the system into *I'm going to the Sporting Club* mode may just not seem worth it, so the system freezes (or *fossilizes*) at the *I go...* stage. It may not seem like a big deal. As Hamdi implies: *go, going, went* – they're just little words that mean roughly the same thing. But there is reason to believe that if the system locks at the *I go...* stage, it may have a knock-on effect, such that a whole range of emergent grammatical structures are effectively 'turned off' too. The learner who gets stuck on saying *I go* instead of *I'm going* is as likely to get stuck on saying *I no like* instead of *I don't like*, and *I am student* rather than *I am a student*. Again, none of these errors is critical, in a strictly communicative sense, but their combined effect may seriously prejudice the learner who needs English for more than just buying bus tickets.

Discovery activity

What do you think is the best approach to take, in order that fossilization doesn't occur?

1 Teach Hamdi the grammar rules of English and make sure he practises them until he gets them right?
2 Correct him every time he makes a mistake?
3 Give him books and tapes for exposure to language in context?
4 Send him to an English-speaking country for a couple of months?
5 All of the above?
6 None of the above?

Commentary ■ ■ ■

A great deal of ink has been expended on this question, and anybody reading the literature on second language acquisition (SLA) might be forgiven for thinking that we have been going round in circles for much of the time. At first grammar was in, then it was out, and now it is back in again. Ditto correction. Ditto immersion: once it was thought that immersion (option 4 above) was the answer; then immersion went out of fashion. Ditto 'comprehensible input' (option 3). In fact, it seems that if the pendulum swings towards options 1 and 2, it swings away from options 3 and 4. And vice versa. In other words, there is a tension between what might be called *instruction plus* solutions, and *instruction minus* solutions – what some writers call *learning*, on the one hand, and *acquisition*, on the other. Certain beliefs and procedures tend to be associated with either one or the other:

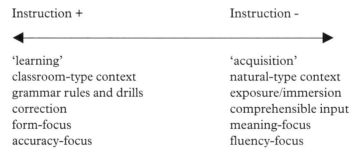

Instruction +	Instruction -
'learning'	'acquisition'
classroom-type context	natural-type context
grammar rules and drills	exposure/immersion
correction	comprehensible input
form-focus	meaning-focus
accuracy-focus	fluency-focus

Most practising teachers tend to situate themselves somewhere along a line between the two extremes. Where does your own position lie? ■

Form-focus versus meaning-focus

As suggested in the diagram above, correction is associated with *instruction plus* solutions. It is also associated with *form* – getting the forms right for the meanings that are intended. Thus, when I attempted to jog Hamdi's memory regarding the forms *go* and *going* it wasn't that I didn't understand what he meant. It was simply that I didn't accept the way his meaning was formed. This is what correction typically means: I understand what you mean, but that's not the way you say it. This is what is meant by a *focus on form*. The alternative – which is associated with *instruction minus* approaches – is a focus on the message, a focus on *meaning*. But does a *focus on meaning* mean no correction?

Here is an imaginary but not untypical exchange between a teacher and student:

T What did you do at the weekend, Ana?
S I go to the mountains.
T Oh, really? Did you go alone?
S No, I go with my friend.
T How nice. What did you do?
S We go skiing...

Notice that the student consistently makes a mistake in situations where the past tense (*went*) is obligatory. The teacher has chosen not to correct her, adopting, instead, a purely conversational style, perhaps because it is the beginning-of-lesson chat stage. The focus is entirely on the *message*. What would be the effect if all the teacher's exchanges with the student were as uncritical? Without any signals to the contrary, it is quite possible that the student's capacity to make the necessary changes to her mental grammar would simply shut down. It's as if the brain were to say 'They obviously understand me out there, so there's nothing more to be learned.'

This, then, is the argument for *negative feedback* – for correction and a focus on form. A focus exclusively on *meaning* may not be enough to trigger the reorganization of the learner's internal grammar. (The technical term for this process is called *restructuring*, and we will be looking at it in more detail in Chapter 4.) Simply communicating with each other in pairs or groups is unlikely to push learners into uncharted territory. Students can get very good at communicating using only minimal resources. What is required, as well as the meaning-focus, is a form-focus, a focus on the language itself, on the medium and not just the message.

≫ p46

So, how is this focus on form engineered? Compare the following exchange with the one above.

T What did you do at the weekend, Ana?
S I go to the mountains.
T Not *go*. What's the past of *go*?
S *goed*?
T No, it's irregular. Look *(writes on board)*: go → went
S I went to the mountains.
T Good. Juan, what did you do at the weekend?

The teacher's two interventions are examples of negative feedback. They unambiguously signal a mistake. As such, they send a clear message to the brain that some restructuring is called for. But what happened to the conversation? With the teacher firmly in the role of 'inquisitor' it is not going to make much headway. The problem of this kind of fairly heavy-handed approach to focusing on form is that it shifts the attention on to 'getting things right', which is not the ideal mindset for exploring the communicative possibilities of a new language. (Witness Hamdi's impatient reaction to my well-meant attempt to correct him!)

Now, compare the last two exchanges with this one:

T What did you do at the weekend, Ana?
S I go to the mountains.

T *Last* weekend, I mean.
S Last weekend, I... erm... *went* to the mountains.
T Did you go alone?
S No, I go with my friend.
T You *went* with your friend?
S Yes, I went with my friend.

In this case, the teacher's intention is to nudge the student to self-correct without interrupting the flow of the talk: a case of *intervening* but not interfering. In the first case, the teacher signals to the student that her utterance is in some way unclear or ambiguous. It may not be the case that the meaning is really unclear – the teacher is simply pretending that it is. The student gets the message that she needs to fine-tune her utterance (to *grammaticize* it) in order to clear up the difficulty.

In the second instance, the teacher *recasts* the student's utterance, as if simply checking, but with sufficient emphasis to draw the student's attention to the error. Thus, the focus on form is engineered without disrupting the flow of the talk: an overall focus on the message is maintained throughout, even if the meaning has to be negotiated a little. The research into the effects of these kinds of feedback devices is quite encouraging. Moreover, it seems quite natural. After all, negotiation of meaning is what happens in genuine communication breakdowns, where form–meaning matches collapse altogether, for example:

S1 How long are you staying here?
S2 Three weeks.
S1 Oh, so you were here for New Year?
S2 No, I arrive yesterday.
S1 But you say you are here since three weeks.
S2 No, I *will* be here for three weeks! You ask me how long I am staying! etc.

Student 1 had intended to ask a question about the past (*How long have you been here?*) but selected a form that is used to talk about the future. The effect of choosing the incorrect form caused a temporary communication breakdown. It has been argued that experiencing such breakdowns and their subsequent repair is an ideal platform for learning. The system is 'shocked' into restructuring itself. Therefore, misunderstanding (or pretending to misunderstand) may be a useful teaching strategy. It is a way of showing how form and meaning are powerfully (as opposed to trivially) interrelated.

It may be the case, however, that the student (Ana) doesn't recognize these veiled prompts to self-correction, and simply interprets them as a certain denseness on the part of the teacher:

T What did you do at the weekend, Ana?
S I go to the mountains.
T *Last* weekend?
S Yes.
T Did you go alone?
S No, I go with my friend.
T You *went* with your friend?
S Yes, I go with my friend, we go skiing.

In this case, the teacher uses conversational-style prompts but the student doesn't take the bait. Here we have a classic case of not noticing: perhaps because the student is not *ready* to notice, or she is too focused on getting her meaning across, or because the teacher's feedback signals are *too* subtle. Or all three.

The same obstinate refusal to notice corrections occurs in children learning their first language, as this example[1] demonstrates:

Child: Want other one spoon, Daddy.
Father: You mean, you want the other spoon.
Child: Yes, I want other one spoon, please Daddy.
Father: Can you say 'the other spoon'?
Child: Other... one... spoon.
Father: Say 'other'.
Child: Other.
Father: 'Spoon'.
Child: Spoon.
Father: 'Other spoon'.
Child: Other... spoon. Now give me other one spoon?

As we said earlier, learners have one-track minds: when they are focused on meaning, they find it very difficult to focus on form. And yet, unless they focus on form, there is a danger that their capacity to restructure will close down. The great challenge of teaching, then, is to set up activities which are essentially meaning-focused, but within which a focus on form can be engineered. It means finding a position that accommodates both *instruction minus* and *instruction plus*. It is an enormously delicate balancing act. It is what makes teaching an *art*, not a science.

Noticing

In the last teacher–student scenario above, I suggested that the student didn't *notice* the subtle corrections that the teacher was offering. The notion of *noticing* is a key one in the study of second language acquisition. Have you ever had the experience, for example, of being taught a new word in a second language, and subsequently seeing it everywhere? It must have been there before, but you simply didn't *notice* it. The importance of *noticing* in language learning was first suggested by a researcher called Richard Schmidt[2]. Schmidt went to Brazil with the intention of learning Portuguese. While there he kept a diary of his language-learning experience. One effect of the Portuguese classes he initially enrolled in was that they seemed to prime him to *notice* things later, when he was simply chatting with friends:

> *Journal entry, Week 6*
>
> *This week we were introduced to and drilled on the imperfect. Very useful!... Wednesday night A came over to play cards... I noticed that his speech was full of the imperfect, which I never heard (or understood) before, and during the evening I managed to produce quite a few myself, without hesitating much. Very satisfying!*

Discovery activity

Reflect on your own experiences of noticing when learning a second language. For example, while writing this chapter, I happened to notice the expression *¡Ni se te occura!* in a comic strip in a Spanish newspaper I was reading. The context suggested that this might mean *Don't even think of it!* I checked this with a friend who confirmed my hypothesis, but who was surprised that I hadn't heard this expression before. Sure enough, the very next day I came across the expression in an interview in a magazine. Now I am waiting for an opportunity to try it out!

Schmidt concluded that classroom instruction was useful because it helped him notice things in the natural input he was exposed to. He also suspected that simply being taught and drilled a form was not enough: he needed to notice it being used naturally. In other words, the two types of experience (*instruction plus* and *instruction minus*) seemed to complement each other quite neatly. Without the formal instruction, specific features of naturally-occurring language use might have washed right over him. But without the real-life interaction, the outcomes of formal instruction may have simply sat on a shelf in the brain and gathered dust. What's more, Schmidt insisted that both kinds of learning required a degree of *attention*. In other words, language learning involves *conscious* processes.

How does all this apply to my student Hamdi? What does he need to notice? And what is my role (ie the teacher's role) in the process?

For a start, Hamdi needs to notice the way the present continuous (*I'm going...*) is preferred when talking about activities in progress. As a teacher, I can help by trying to focus Hamdi's attention on this feature of the target language in the input that he is exposed to.

But Hamdi also needs to notice that his communicatively acceptable *I go...* is not what a more proficient speaker of English would use in this instance. So, as a teacher I need to provide opportunities for Hamdi to become aware of the distance to be covered between the present state of his second language (his *interlanguage*) and the target forms of that language.

To summarize: in order to learn a language
- learners must pay attention to linguistic features of the input that they are exposed to
- learners must *notice the gap*, ie they must make comparisons between the current state of their knowledge, as realized in their output, and the target language system, available as input.

One way to get Hamdi to notice the gap is to give him feedback when he makes a mistake. But, as we saw earlier, this is a tricky business. Too much correction, and the learner shuts up. Too little – or too subtle – and the learner simply doesn't notice. And the system shuts down. One possibility is to encourage learners to compare their output on a specific task with the output of a more proficient speaker on the same task. This is » pp21–30 the principle behind the *grammaring* activities we looked at in Chapter 2.

Consciousness-raising

Providing learners with feedback on their output is one way of raising their awareness about the current state of their language acquisition, but sometimes a pre-emptive strike may be what's called for. Activities designed to make students aware of features of the language – to *notice* them – are called *consciousness-raising* activities. Traditionally, such consciousness-raising was mediated by the teacher's explanations and presentations.

Here, for example, is an activity designed to introduce Hamdi to the present continuous (*I am going...*), which, as we saw, he fails to use in contexts where it is appropriate (*I am going to the Sporting Club*). Read it and decide how useful it might be.

T *(writes on board: 'the present continuous – I am going...'):*   The present continuous is formed by the auxiliary verb *be* plus the present participle. We use the present continuous to describe things happening now. For example, *the sun is shining*. Is that clear?

Crystal clear, but perhaps not a lot of use to Hamdi. Apart from the lack of context there are some tricky ideas and terms to process (remember Hamdi is not a fluent English speaker – not yet). And where is Hamdi in all this? Probably thinking of the tennis match he's playing after class.

OK, then, what about this as an alternative?

T Watch me. *(walks across room)* I am walking across the room. I am walking. I am walking. I am walking. What am I doing?

S You are walking.

T Good. Everyone, repeat.

Ss You are walking.

Here the teacher is attempting to shortcut the explanations by using actions to associate a form (the present continuous) with a meaning (activity in progress). But he could just as easily – and correctly – say *I walk across the room*. Is this little bit of theatre really going to get to the heart of Hamdi's problem?

OK. Here is another one. The teacher draws two stick figures on the board. He names one Chris and the other Kim. He tells the class that one day Chris meets Kim in the street. Kim is carrying a tennis racquet. The teacher says: 'Chris says to Kim "Hi Kim, where are you going?" Kim says "I'm going to the club."' 'OK,' says the teacher, 'repeat: I'm going to the club. Everybody: I'm going to the club.' Class repeat in unison.

Well, we seem to be getting somewhere. We have a situation. We have a context. We have natural-sounding language. We would seem to have all the necessary ingredients to guarantee that the students, including Hamdi, can make the connection from the classroom context (the context of learning) to the real-life context (the context of use), when and wherever it occurs.

We could, of course, further improve this presentation by role-playing it in front of the class, by making a recording of the encounter, by showing a video of it with professional actors acting out the roles, and so on. But, the problem may not be with the method of presentation at all. It may lie in the idea of presentation itself. As every experienced teacher knows, the clarity and relevance of the presentation are no guarantee that the transfer from classroom to real-life will take place. There is something about language learning which seems to confound the best laid plans of teachers. It's as if the human mind had – well – a mind of its own.

In fact, it's not just teachers who have discovered this. Researchers have been saying for some time now that you can lead a student to grammar but you can't make him learn; that the process of learning (a language at least) is not a mechanistic, linear, input-output one. It seems to be much more capricious than that. As one researcher, Diane Larsen-Freeman[3], put it:

> Learning linguistic items is not a linear process – learners do not master one item and then move on to another. In fact, the learning curve for a single item is not linear either. The curve is filled with peaks and valleys, progress and backslidings.

In this sense, language development is more organic than mechanistic – an argument that will be explored in Chapter 4. Such a view has meant that there is less faith than there used to be in the *presentation* and *practice* of language rules: they are no guarantee of a smooth run through the language-learning process.

So, why should consciousness-raising be any different? The difference is basically one of reduced expectations. With consciousness-raising there is not the expectation of immediate and consistently accurate production – the assumption underlying a presentation-type methodology. The aim of consciousness-raising is to provide the kind of data that is likely to become *intake*, which, when the time is right, will have the effect of triggering the restructuring of the learner's mental grammar. To use a metaphor, consciousness-raising is like a slow-release pill that affects the system over time. The effects may not even be very direct. As Schmidt found, being taught the Portuguese imperfect primed him to notice it when his friend came round; his noticing it a few times was the incentive to use it. This is a different view of learning than implied by presentation-practice, which assumes a direct link between input and output, between teaching and learning. The two views can be represented like this:

1 PP (Presentation + Practice)

   input ➞ output

2 C-R (Consciousness-raising)

   input ➞ noticing ➞ intake ➞ output

Meaning and form together

As we saw with correction, the best kind of feedback is probably the kind of feedback that sends a signal to the student that their message is unclear or ambiguous – not simply because the message is ill-formed, but because the form sends out a different message than the one the student had intended.

It follows that the best sort of consciousness-raising activities should also attempt to raise the learner's awareness as to how form and meaning are connected – not through tedious explanation, or even demonstration, but in such a way that the connection is seen to *matter*.

It seems to be the case that, unless the learner notices *the effect that grammatical choices have on meaning*, then the noticing is not sufficient to have any long-term effects on restructuring. To notice the effect of grammatical choices on meaning assumes that the focus is on meaning to start with. The frequent and repetitive occurrence of a language item during an activity is not enough. Learners need to realize why the choice of that item – as opposed to the choice of another, or zero choice – *matters*.

Here, for example, is part of a classroom exchange that happened when I was presenting and practising the present perfect to a class of adult students, again in Egypt. We are practising the previously taught pattern *Have you done X yet?*, using prompts I am supplying:

Me:	Visit the Pyramids. Hisham?
Hisham:	Have you visited the Pyramids yet?
Me:	Good. Eat kebab. Mervat?
Mervat:	Have you eaten kebab yet?
Me:	Good. See oriental dancer. Magdi?
Magdi:	Have you seen an oriental dancer yet?
Me:	Good. Hear Om Kalthoum [a well known Egyptian singer]. Hoda?
Hoda:	Have you heard Om Kalthoum yet?
Me:	Good...
Hisham	*surprised by this reference to 'insider' cultural knowledge and interrupting to ask a 'real' question)*: Did you hear Om Kalthoum, Mr Scott?
Me:	Hisham! *What* are we practising?!

How is it that the student (Hisham) seemed incapable of retrieving the correct form (ie the present perfect: *Have you heard Om Kalthoum?*) for the meaning he wished to express, when the form would seem to have been optimally available? The sole purpose of the drill was for students to practise the form of the present perfect. Yet as soon as the student's attention shifted to the expression of a real meaning, the form went out the window, and he reverted to a kind of default setting: the past simple. The reason is probably due to the fact that the drill required no decision-making at any but the most superficial level. It did not allow the student to appreciate the effect on meaning of the 'marked' form (the present perfect) over the default form (the past simple). The present perfect wasn't made to *matter*. And, not mattering, it wasn't noticed.

Compare the drill above, with this activity:

The teacher draws two stick figures on the board and establishes that one is Ben and one is Betty. Ben is back in the UK after a three-week holiday in Egypt. Betty is half-way through her three-week holiday in Egypt. The teacher is having a three-way conversation with Ben and Betty by phone.

T Ben, did you see the Pyramids?
(indicates that Ben answers 'Yes')

T Betty, have you seen the Pyramids yet?
(indicates that she, too, answers 'Yes')
(The teacher writes both these sentences on the board, then invites the class to tell him who he is speaking to – Ben or Betty?)

T Have you been to Aswan yet? (Answer: Betty)
Did you eat falafel? (Answer: Ben)
Did you go sailing on the Nile? (Answer: Ben)
Have you been sailing on the Nile? (Answer: Betty)
Did you learn any Arabic? (Answer: Ben)
Did you ride a camel? (Answer: Ben)
Have you learnt any Arabic? (Answer: Betty)

To do this activity, the students have to attend to the form (ie whether it's past simple or present perfect) in order to perform a task which is essentially a meaning-focused task, ie who is the teacher speaking to? The exercise is so contrived that the only clue they have is the form of the verb phrase. In this way the form of the verb is made to matter.

Did that last exercise seem a little *too* contrived? Well, here is an alternative:

The teacher tells the class that they are going to listen to some answerphone messages that he (the teacher) has just received. All the messages are from friends who are on holiday or who have just returned from holiday. The students' first task is to guess which city or country each message refers to. Here are the messages:

- Hi, Joe. How are you? Great holiday! We've been to the Louvre and the Eiffel Tower, but we haven't been to Versailles yet. We'll phone you back. Bye.
- Joe, it's Barry. Fantastic holiday! We went everywhere – the Colisseum, St Peters, Hadrian's Villa – and we had great Italian food. Speak to you soon. Bye.
- Hi, Joe, Cathy here. How was your holiday? I went sightseeing and shopping and spent a fortune. Didn't have time to see Big Ben! But I bought you a fab T-shirt. Bye.
- Joe, baby! Donald speaking. Amazing holiday. Taj Mahal, Rajahstan. I've travelled thousands of miles, all by train. Third class. And I've met some really interesting people. I've even seen a tiger! Money running out, have to go...
- Hello, Joe. It's six o'clock Tuesday evening. Just phoning to tell you about my trip. I had a great time. I climbed to the top of Ayers' Rock, can you believe it! And I went surfing at Bondi Beach. But I never made it to Cairns. I have some great photos to show you. Well, speak to you soon. Bye.

Having checked the first task, the teacher then asks the students to listen again and tell him which of his friends are still on holiday and which are back home.

Here we have an activity that is, for all intents and purposes, almost wholly meaning-focused. The first task, designed to familiarize students with the text, is relatively easy and simply requires students to pick out a few proper names. The second task is much more subtle and cannot be done without paying attention to the verb forms: are they past simple (thereby situating the holiday in a period of time unconnected to the present), or are they in the present perfect (implying a period of time that is connected to the present)? For students who are unfamiliar with, or unsure of, this distinction, the task forces them to *notice* it. Again, there are no other clues in the text to help them.

Grammar interpretation activities

Both the preceding activities belong to a class of consciousness-raising tasks that are called either *grammar interpretation activities* or *structured input tasks*. The principles underlying them have been elaborated by the writer and researcher Rod Ellis[4]. Ellis supports the view that *comprehension* is a prerequisite for acquisition, and preferably comprehension without immediate production. Forcing production of a newly learned item too soon (as in the presentation–practice model) may be counter-productive, in that the effort involved in articulation diverts attention away from simply understanding how the new item works: a case of getting-your-tongue-round-it at the expense of getting-your-mind-round-it. And, as we have seen, the processes of restructuring run deep and are not necessarily instant nor direct. There is a body of research that lends support to this view. Hence, the two tasks above (about holidays) require students simply to listen and understand. This is why they are called grammar *interpretation* activities.

Look, for example, at this task:

Task 1   Choose the appropriate form of the verb in these texts:

a) Jack Kerouac (1922–69), the American writer, _____ (spend) much of his life travelling the USA. He also _____ (visit) Mexico and North Africa. He _____ (write) a number of novels including *On The Road* (1957), which _____ (sell) a million copies in Kerouac's lifetime.

b) Gary Snyder (1930–), the American poet, _____ (spend) his childhood in Oregon. He then _____ (study) Japanese and Chinese at the University of California. From 1956 to 68 he _____ (live) in Japan. Since then, he _____ (live) in California. He _____ (do) many different jobs in his life: seaman, logger, carpenter among others. He _____ (write) a number of books of poetry, including *Myths and Texts*, which _____ (be) published in 1960.

It is a classic grammar practice task (and not a bad one, either), in which students choose the correct form of the verb to fill the gap. The choice of verb form depends on their understanding of the context. The fact that Kerouac is dead and Snyder is alive will, in some cases, determine a different choice of verb form (past simple or present perfect). Thus:

(Kerouac) *wrote* a number of novels...

(Snyder) *has written* a number of books...

Note that the students have to *produce* the target form. It is not a case of simply interpreting it. However, notice how the following task differs:

Task 2   Here are two US writers:

Jack Kerouac   Gary Snyder

(1922–1969)   (1930–)

■ Can you complete these sentences, with either Kerouac or Snyder?

a) _____ was born in 1930.

b) _____ died in 1969.

c) _____ was a writer.

d) _____ wrote several novels as well as poetry.

e) _____ is a poet.

f) _____ has written many books of poetry.

g) _____ lived in USA, Mexico and Tangier.

h) _____ has lived in USA and Japan.

i) _____ has done many different jobs – seaman, logger, carpenter among others.

j) _____ has been married for 28 years.

k) _____ never married.

In this task, students do not have to produce the targeted verb forms; they simply have to understand their significance. This, then, is a true grammar interpretation activity. On the assumption that understanding precedes production, it would make more sense to start with this activity and then follow with Task 1 above, although not necessarily immediately. On the 'slow release' principle, it might be better to delay the production task, but not so long that students forget the interpretation task. It has been suggested that learning is 'remembering understanding something'. If this is the case, then the two activities could complement each other neatly.

Ellis[4] identifies three main goals for grammar interpretation tasks:
1 To enable learners to identify the meaning(s) realized by a specific grammatical feature;
2 To enhance input in such a way that learners are induced to notice a grammatical feature that otherwise they might ignore;
3 To enable learners to notice the gap between the way a particular form works to convey meaning and the way they themselves are using it.

He is cautious about making strong claims for these task types, being a scientist by disposition. Nevertheless, there seems to be a good deal of sound theory to support their use. Anything that promotes noticing, after all, must be of enormous benefit to the learner.

Summary

We started this chapter by emphasizing the importance of consciousness, and in particular of *noticing*, in language acquisition. Learners need to notice features of the input – specifically the way that the choice of form impacts on meaning. They also need to notice how far they have to travel to achieve target-like grammaring: they need to notice the gap. Unless their awareness is raised in these two ways, it is unlikely that restructuring of their mental grammar will occur, in which case it may stabilize into a less than fully grammaticized state.

We have also looked at ways a focus on form can be integrated into activities that are essentially message-focused. One way is by providing feedback on the effectiveness of the learner's message-making, even if, at times, we have to pretend we don't understand. Another activity is the grammar interpretation task, a way of enhancing input so as to optimize noticing. In Chapter 2 we looked at grammaticization tasks, which are output oriented. In the next chapter we will take a closer look at restructuring and integrate it into a view of language learning that sees grammar(ing) as being an emergent phenomenon – something that, like a tree, just grows. Such a view has important implications for the teacher's role, and we will be looking at those implications in more detail in Chapter 5.

References

1 Braine, M. 'The acquisition of language in infant and child.' In Reed, C. (ed.) 1971 *The Learning of Language*. Appleton-Century-Crofts. Quoted in Yule, G. 1985 *The Study of Language*. Cambridge: Cambridge University Press

2 Schmidt, R. and Frota, S. 'Developing basic conversational ability in a second language: A case study of an adult learner of Portuguese.' In Day, R. (ed.) 1986 *Talking to learn: Conversation in second language acquisition*. Rowley, MA: Newbury House

3 Larsen-Freeman, D. 1997 'Chaos/Complexity science and second language acquisition.' In *Applied Linguistics 18*, no. 2, pp141-65

4 Ellis, R. 1997 *SLA Research and Language Teaching*. Oxford: Oxford University Press, pp152-3

Chapter 4 **Emergent grammar**

The approaches to grammar teaching that have been outlined so far imply a view of learning that is less the accumulation of facts ('learning the grammar') than a process of growth and unfolding ('grammaring'). Metaphors of growth and unfolding find echoes in current scientific theories of complexity and bio-ecology. In this chapter we will explore those connections, before (in Chapter 5) suggesting how such metaphors of growth and emergence might be realized in classroom practice.

'Doing the present perfect'

The argument of this book has been that, from a psychological perspective, grammar is less a *thing* than something that we *do*: it is a process. Learning, producing and understanding language involve engaging in processes of 'grammaring'. This contrasts with a product view of grammar, which construes grammar as an 'out there' phenomenon: a body of facts about the language that have to be learned and then taken down off the shelf, so to speak, every time an utterance is produced or interpreted.

The product-process distinction, of course, has implications for teaching. A product view of grammar lends itself to a *transmission* style of teaching. If grammar is simply a set of facts about the language, then the teacher's job is to transmit these facts and the learner is expected to internalize and apply them.

Discovery activity

Here are three teachers talking about lessons they have just taught. To what extent are their lesson descriptions consistent with a transmission style of teaching?

Teacher 1

'My last class was level 5 upper-intermediate, a class of seven or eight students. I revised the second and third conditionals and would *and* should, *which they found extremely difficult. They're a bad class and I've dropped back two levels to level 3 listening, so I did level 3 listening, which they found quite difficult, and we did discussion for 5 or 10 minutes on human cloning, which went quite well because they were all interested.'*

Teacher 2

'It was first level, daily routines, verbs, get up, go to work, get to work, *third person* s *and that's about it.'*

'And what happened exactly?'

'Presented the verbs, did some pron, ahh, flash cards, students ordered the flash cards, practised third person s *and did a listening at the end.'*

Teacher 3

'We started the lesson off with a game, 'For, since and ago'. *Then we did a game of miming jobs. Then we did a listening to introduce... we were talking about what jobs we would like, what jobs we wouldn't like to do, and if we would like to open a restaurant, and then we discussed the advantages and disadvantages of a restaurant, and then we listened to a girl who'd just given up her job to open up a restaurant and the advantages and disadvantages and it was to introduce* have to *as an obligation and the difference between* have *as a possession and* have to *as an obligation.'*

Commentary ■ ■ ■

Notice how the teachers 'reify' grammar – that is, they treat it as a thing – a commodity that is transmitted (or *presented*, or *introduced*) to the learners. 'I revised the second and third conditionals...'; '[I] presented the verbs, did some pron...'. Even Teacher 3, whose lesson revolves around a listening text, uses the text as a vehicle for the delivery of a pre-selected grammar item. Notice, also, that it is not just grammar that is 'thing-ed'. The teachers talk about *doing a listening*, *doing a discussion*, *doing a game*, rather than simply *listening*, *discussing* and *playing*. In other words, the lesson is parcelled up into activities, and the activities in turn *contain* the grammar that is being delivered. According to this view, teaching is like a mail delivery system or a factory production line.

At this point, you might like to think of alternative ways of talking about grammar teaching. In the next chapter I will provide examples of possible alternatives. ■

Covering grammar

As well as 'doing' grammar, teachers often talk about 'covering' grammar: 'In this course we will *cover* the first and second conditionals.' Again, this is consistent with a view of grammar as being a number of points or units or items, the accumulation of which results in language proficiency. The 'grammar points' metaphor is popular with ELT publishers, too, as these extracts from their catalogues suggest:

> English structures are presented in small, manageable units and in incremental steps...

> There is a clearly defined and limited grammatical and lexical syllabus. New language is introduced gradually and methodically, and consolidated through a variety of controlled practice activities...

> Offering systematic coverage of all the key items of English grammar needed by secondary and adult students...

The same bite-sized view of grammar is reflected in the advice given to teachers in Teacher's Books:

> Low-level language learners require a very logical, step-by-step approach...[1]

> By the end of Level 1, students will have learnt to express themselves simply but correctly in the present, past and future...[2]

(If only my student Hamdi (in Chapter 3) had had access to this last book! The *I go to the club* conversation might never have happened.)

Of course, grammar-as-thing lends itself to syllabusing and to testing. It is easier to devise a programme or design a test if what you are programming or testing is packageable into bite-sized units – like grammar McNuggets! It is less easy to syllabus or measure something fluid, in motion and with unfixed boundaries. Grammar as a psychological process is much more slippery than grammar as a list of facts.

But, unfortunately, the grammar McNuggets delivery system doesn't seem to match the way language is actually acquired – not if we take the evidence from language acquisition research seriously. Nor does it match the experience of many classroom teachers, frustrated at the seeming inability of learners to learn the building blocks of language in a step-by-step way. (How many teachers have been heard to complain to their students, 'But we did this last week! We covered this yesterday!') It appears that the process of learning is a lot messier than a step-by-step model suggests.

Discovery activity

Here is a list of grammar structures. According to a step-by-step view of language learning, what do you think would be the most logical order to teach them in? Alternatively, divide them into beginners, intermediate and more advanced structures.

present simple (*I go*)

past simple: irregular verbs (*we went*)

past simple: regular verbs (*the party ended*)

past passive (*it was organized*)

time adverbials (*in the afternoon, at night*)

defining relative clauses (*the club where I go*)

infinitive of purpose (*we went to visit*)

adverbial clauses of time (*when I was on holiday*)

existential there (*there was a party*)

prepositional phrases of place (*in a restaurant, on the beach*)

Now, read this composition by an elementary level student. Which of the above structures does he get right? Which does he attempt but get wrong?

> *The Best Party*
>
> *Last summer when I was on holidays, in the social club where I going during all weekends of year, had had a beautiful party. I went whit my family and the same friends. It were to organized for to celebration 25th birthday it.*
>
> *First day we went by bus with a guide for to visit Tarragona arounds. During the travel we stoped for to lunch in a good restaurant on the beach coast. At the afternoon we were visit Charlie Rivel home in Cubellas a smal town. At the night after dinner we went together the Arnau Theatre Show in Barcelona.*
>
> *Second day at the morning we were in the partner delivery presents. It delivery finished with a shellfish.*
>
> *The party ended at the night with a big dinner and a beautiful danced for all partners.*

Commentary ■ ■ ■

It is interesting that the student makes mistakes with grammar structures that are traditionally associated with beginners' level syllabuses, while correctly using structures that are normally taught much later. For example, he makes a mistake with the present simple (*going* instead of *go*), fails to use existential *there* (*There was a party*), and has a lot of trouble with time adverbials, overgeneralizing *at the* (*at the night, at the morning*): all fairly elementary structures. On the other hand, he uses the past simple accurately (both regular and irregular) and employs a number of relatively sophisticated syntactic structures such as a defining relative clause (*in the social club where I going*) and an adverbial clause of time (*when I was on holidays*). This may simply be a case of positive transfer from Catalan (the student's first language), but this doesn't entirely account for the flawed passive construction *it were to organized* or the curious *had had a party*. Maybe we have to conclude that the learner's acquisition order bears only a loose, even accidental, relationship with either the order of grammar instruction or his first language.

Restructuring

The process of learning, I am arguing, is slippery and messy – not the step-by-step, one-thing-at-a-time process enshrined in coursebook syllabuses. In fact, it is sometimes the case that certain features of the grammar seem to get worse before they get better. A case in point is the learning of irregular past tense forms, such as *ate, went, bought*, etc. Typically, learners go through four, possibly five, stages in their acquisition of these forms:

1 They use the one form for both present and past   *eat* (or *eating*)
2 They start to produce correct past forms   *ate*
3 They attach the regular past ending to the verb   *eated*
4 They may even produce a mixture of regular and irregular   *ated*
5 They consistently produce the correct form   *ate*

In other words learners may go through a phase of producing correct forms (stage 2), and then seem to regress – a case of two steps forward and one step back, or what is known as a *U-shaped learning curve*. What seems to be happening is that learners pick up the correct form (*ate*) simply through having been exposed to it, learning it as a word in its own right, not as the past tense of something else. Then they start to notice that many past tense verbs have *-ed* on the end. They overgeneralize this rule and apply it to irregular verbs: hence *eated* and *ated* (stages 3 and 4). This is a good example of the way the mental grammar reorganizes itself to accommodate new data: a process that is called *restructuring*.

Developmental orders, such as the one described above, are not restricted to verb endings. A number of sequences have been identified that lend support to the view that the learner's mental grammar follows predictable paths. Take the example of negation: the following represents the developmental route that learners typically traverse on their way to the target form *He doesn't eat meat*.

1 He no eat meat.

2 He not eat meat.

3 He don't eat meat.

4 He doesn't eat meat.

Rod Ellis[3] comments:

> The way along this route is a gradual one. Some learners can take longer than two years and some never travel the whole distance. The stages are not clearly defined but overlap considerably. Development does not consist of sudden jumps, but of the gradual reordering of early rules in favour of later ones.

Yet all learners seem to follow the same path. So predictable (hence systematic) are these developmental routes that it seems valid to talk about the learners having a grammar of their own – the *learner's* grammar – as opposed to the target grammar, ie the one found in grammar books.

The learner's grammar is not a deviant or impoverished form of grammar. It has its own integrity, its own rules, its own internal consistency. It also has its own contextual legitimacy – in other words, in certain contexts it is as effective, or even more effective, than the target model, as this example, from a newspaper advertisement demonstrates:

Now is time for communicate for everybody!!!!

Everybody like make new friend!!! Now is time for communicate for everybody. If you like communicate, is very easy in modern world. You can make smartgroup and join with old or new friend in many country. Or even for club or work.

For share of ideas and information! For some discussion! For free....... This what internet really is about.

Everything is for peace, friendship, huminity and love.

www.smartgroups.com

The learner's grammar is dynamic – it is constantly changing and evolving in the direction of the target grammar. (The fact that the target is constantly shifting adds another element of mystery to the whole process.) It is a *process* grammar, in the same way that a germinating seed is a plant in the process of becoming. And, like a plant, the learner's grammar needs nurturing – it needs the right conditions for growth and emergence. It needs uncovering.

Note: *un*covering, not covering. A simplistic response to the evidence of a 'natural order' of acquisition would be to design syllabuses that reflect this natural order – syllabuses that would *cover* the grammar, but in the order in which learners naturally acquire it. But, for a start, this would mean including non-standard forms in the syllabus (*She eated. He no eat meat*), which not only runs counter to common sense, but does not reflect the kind of language naturalistic (ie non-classroom) learners are exposed to in the real world. More importantly, it credits to syllabuses more influence than they in fact have. It assumes that the simple act of including an item on a syllabus and then teaching it somehow magically causes its acquisition. It attempts to impose on a complex phenomenon a simple cause-and-effect principle. But language learning is not simple.

Complex systems

We have seen how the learner's grammar restructures itself as it responds to incoming data. There seem to be periods of little change alternating with periods of a great deal of flux and variability, and even some backsliding. In this way, process grammars are not unlike other complex systems which fluctuate between chaotic states and states of relative stability.

In fact, the similarities between language and other complex systems – such as the weather or the flocking behaviour of birds or fluctuations in commodity markets – are starting to attract the attention of linguists. They argue that language and, in particular, language learning, share the following features with other complex systems: they are

- dynamic and non-linear
- adaptive and feedback sensitive
- self-organizing
- emergent

Language is dynamic and non-linear

Complex systems are dynamic: they are in a state of constant change and movement. Think of the weather, or a shoal of fish, or a crowd at a football match: each is in a state of constant flux. Moreover, they change and move in ways that cannot always be predicted by looking at their individual components. That is, complex systems do not behave in a simple, linear and deterministic way, where a small change in one element of the system causes a knock-on and predictable effect in another, and so on. Rather, small effects in complex systems may precipitate major changes. And vice versa. The much-quoted 'butterfly' effect is an example of this: a butterfly flaps its wings in one part of the world and sets in motion events that lead to a storm in another. The next time it flaps its wings nothing of meteorological consequence happens. In similar fashion, it takes just one pebble to precipitate a landslide – but which pebble?

Non-linearity in language learning is exhibited in the way learners move from *ate* to *eated* and back to *ate* again, a pattern that seems to occur irrespective of whatever teaching takes place. This is not to say that the teaching is of no use, but that *small effects of teaching do not seem to have comparable and incremental small effects on learning*. It may in fact be the case that the restructuring of the learner's past tense system is triggered by small effects of *noticing* that have major consequences in terms of the development of the learner's overall mental grammar. The restructuring is like the landslide: in retrospect we can say it was that particular pebble that triggered it, but before the event it is difficult if not impossible to predict it or plan it.

Language is adaptive and feedback-sensitive

The weather is a complex system, but it doesn't 'learn'. An ant-colony, on the other hand, is an example of a complex *adaptive* system, because it is not just complex but it adapts to its environment – it is self-organizing and learning. It is constantly revising and rearranging itself in response to changes around it. Such adaptive mechanisms may be very simple, but the effects are often complex. Thus, the simple mechanisms by which plants and animals have adapted to complex environments have resulted in enormous diversity. But the diversity is not unchecked. The system's sensitivity to feedback means that evolutionary changes do not spiral out of control. Periods of stability are ensured until such times as environmental changes require further adaptations.

The same feedback loop may well apply to language development, both in the way languages have developed over time, and in terms of the acquisition of language by an individual person. From a historical perspective, it sometimes appears that language diversity has spiralled out of control – look at the number of interpreters needed at the United Nations, for example. But, at a local level – in the village or neighbourhood – stability is maintained by strong social and familial pressures to speak the same language, using the same words and the same accent. Similarly, the fact that the learner's language emerges in the direction of the target language – and not off on a side track of its own – may have a lot to do with the pressure, or need, or desire, to conform. Where there is no pressure or need or desire to conform, the learner's system may simply close down. We « pp18–19 saw how this happened in the case of the Italian learner, Santo, in Chapter 2. Later in the chapter we shall be looking at ways of providing the kind of feedback loop that may prevent this kind of fossilization.

Language is self-organizing

Another characteristic of complex systems is their capacity to *self-organize*. Systems that are left to themselves (closed systems) tend to run down – they move from order to stasis, just as an unwound clock will eventually stop. However, open systems – systems that are open to the intake of new energy – may move in the opposite direction, evolving into more complex states. Once a critical point is reached, they reorganize themselves – a characteristic that has been described as 'order for free'. For example, a crowd clapping a rock band will move from unsynchronized to synchronized applause without any apparent cue. The individual and self-interested dealings of investors cause rhythmic fluctuations in the stock markets. And the fact that adjacent lines of cars at toll booths are roughly of equal length is not because their drivers are obeying some rule of the road: simply that out of the sum total of their purely individual goals a pattern emerges. This is described by Murray Gell-Mann[4]:

> The common feature of all these processes is that in each one a complex adaptive system acquires information about its environment and its own interaction with that environment, identifying regularities in that information,

condensing those irregularities into a kind of 'schema' or model, and acting in the real world on the basis of that schema. In each case, there are various competing schemata, and the results of the action in the real world feed back to influence the competition among those schemata.

The above description of self-organization seems to capture very neatly the way language competence evolves, particularly if we substitute *rule(s)* for *schema* (pl. *schemata*). In fact, Gell-Mann uses the acquisition of grammar as an example of a complex adaptive system at work:

> In constructing an internal grammar, a child effectively separates grammatical features from all the other factors [...] that have led to the particular sentences he or she hears. Only in that way is compression into a manageable set of grammatical rules possible.

In other words, the child discovers regularities in the incoming 'data stream' by noticing that parts of the stream have features in common. These regularities are abstracted from the stream and 'compressed' into a schema, or rule. This rule may not be the 'correct' one, nor a very stable one:

> A schema is subject to variation, and the different variants are tried out in the real world. In order to try them out, it is necessary to fill in details, such as the ones that were thrown away in creating the schema... For example, the child may say, 'We sang a hymn yesterday morning.' That sentence passes muster. If, however, the child says, 'I brang home something to show you,' the parent may reply, 'It's very nice of you to show me that cockroach you found at Aunt Bessie's, but you ought to say "I brought home something...".' That experience would probably result in the child's trying out a new schema, one that allows for both sing-sang and bring-brought.

« Chapter 2 p17

We can see this rule-forming, rule-testing and rule-refining process at work in the development of the pronoun system, from

Adam home. Adam go hill.

to

I like drink it. What me doing?

to

That what I do. You watch me.

Initially, no pronoun schema was extracted from the data stream at all. At the second stage the pattern that was abstracted was 'sentence initial position = *I*, thereafter *me*' – a schema that works four times out of five. This schema then competed with, and finally yielded to, a more subtle one that recognizes the distinction between subjects and objects.

Language is emergent

Such patterning is described as *emergent*. The behaviour of a complex system is not built into any one component. Rather, it *emerges* from the interactions of its components. Moreover, the global structure that emerges from the local interactions of individual agents feeds back to influence the behaviour of the individuals. Thus the ability of a flock of birds to swoop and dive as a unitary whole is not because there is one 'leader' bird directing the action. Each bird is interacting only with the birds in its immediate environment: out of the combination of all these local interactions a global pattern emerges, so that the flock seems to work as one. Likewise, the ant colony, faced by a sudden flood or the predations of an ant-eater, reorganizes (restructures) itself – not because of orders from a central command – but as the result of the aggregate behaviour of thousands of individuals interacting locally.

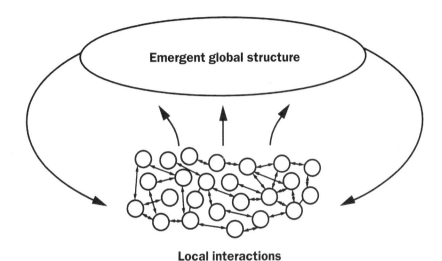

Emergence in complex adaptive systems[5]

Linguists are now saying that the complicated patterns of grammar may be similarly self-organizing and emergent. As we saw in Chapter 2, language development, both in first and second languages, tends to follow a route from a lexical stage to a syntactical one. Initially, lexical items – words and phrases – are picked up and stored fairly randomly. At some point, these individual items start to connect and cohere into patterns (just as the random clapping of lots of people in the audience fuses into a rhythm, or the individual birds in a flock 'link' destinies and swoop and soar together). There seems to be a critical point when the connections between similarly patterned words or phrases become strong enough to 'learn' new forms. To take the example of irregular verbs again: over time, the child stores *sang* as the past of *sing*, and *drank* as the past of *drink*, and *sank* as the past of *sink*. At some point the links between these words strengthen to the point that, faced with *spring*, the child correctly produces *sprang*.

« pp 15–21

Computer scientists working with artificial neural networks have been able to replicate these learning processes. Neural networks resemble the brain in the sense that they consist of a massive collection of elementary but intricately connected nodes. Also like the brain, neural networks work in parallel, with many connections activated simultaneously. (This is unlike a conventional computer which acts in a one-step-at-a-time fashion, or serially.) The network 'learns' by abstracting regularities from input data: the more instances of a pattern in the input, the stronger the connections between nodes in the network. The regularities are not stored as rules, but as connection strengths distributed over a vastly interconnected network. For example, instead of the regular past tense being stored as a general rule ('Add -*ed* to the base form of the verb'), imagine a mental network in which individual verbs (*work*, *play*, *live*, etc) are connected more or less strongly to *-ed*. The network acts *as if* it was working from rules, but in fact these rules are simply the by-products of paths through the connections. It is not the by-products that are stored, but the pathways. In this 'connectionist' model of learning, there are no products, only processes.

Connectionism is still hotly debated, but some of the results of neural network modelling have been impressive. As well as 'learning' irregular verb forms and correctly inducing *sprang* from *spring*, for example, they have also made the same mistakes as a child/learner might, eg producing *brang* from *bring*, and more interestingly still, they have mimicked the two-steps-forward, one-step-backward developmental path typical of human learners (eg producing *eated* after having correctly produced *ate*).

Another capacity such networks have is that, when a number of similar patterns have been stored, the system will respond to the central tendency of the stored patterns, even if the central tendency never appeared in the input data. This is called the 'prototype effect'. It is analogous to inferring the appearance of a robin after having seen only a starling, a parrot and a pelican! Or, to use a language example, the pattern of complex noun phrases (such as *not all of the three famous Andrews sisters*) may become established when the learner has been exposed to only fragments of this pattern: eg *both of the men, two dogs, the Blues Brothers, not half*, etc.

A connectionist view argues that complex language forms are not necessarily the result of complex mental processes. The processes may in fact be very simple, but, with massive exposure to the complexity of language in its social settings, these simple processes may be sufficient to generate language that *looks as if* it is the product of complex rules.

To summarize then: a connectionist view argues that exposure to stretches of language, eg sequences of sounds or of words, triggers simple inferencing operations in the brain, and may even spontaneously generate forms that are not only absent in the input, but are more complex than anything in the input. This has led some researchers to propose theories not of second language *acquisition*, but of second language *emergence*. The grammar is not implanted from outside; rather it emerges out of the encounter between a pattern-hungry brain and a language-rich environment. Moreover, the grammar emerges not as a symbolic system of rules, but as a set of procedures – a process.

A somewhat simplistic illustration of the process might look like this (but remember we are dealing with complexity, so the arrangement of factors is much more complicated than this rather mechanistic diagram suggests):

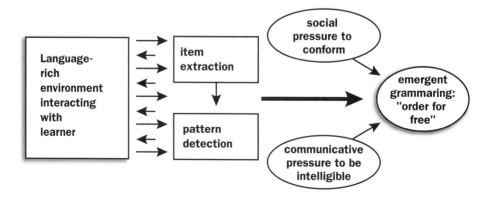

Scaffolding

We have argued that language learning shares features of other complex systems, such as non-linearity, self-organization and emergence. That grammar is an emergent phenomenon, rather than something imposed, also finds support from the study of parent-child interactions, and, by extension, from learner-learner and teacher-learner interactions.

In the following conversation[6] between a child and his mother, the child (Mark, aged two) comments on the fact that the central heating boiler has just ignited:

Mark:	Oh popped on.
Mother:	Pardon?
Mark:	It popped on.
Mother:	It popped on?
Mark:	Yeh.
Mother:	What did?
Mark:	Er – fire on.
Mother:	The fire?
Mark:	Yeh... Pop the... fire popped it fire.
Mother:	Oh yes. The fire popped on, didn't it?

Notice how the mother maintains the conversation by extending and reformulating the child's relatively simple utterances. And notice, too, how, in this supportive framework, the child's utterances increase in complexity and length, as it picks up on the mother's framing language:

popped on ➤ it popped on ➤ pop the... fire popped it fire

We can almost feel 'the fire popped on' struggling to pop out! The supportive framework provided by the mother is called *scaffolding* because that's exactly what it is: a temporary support that makes it possible for children (and second language learners) to participate in social interaction that is beyond their actual developmental level. Here is another example, this time between a teacher and a learner:

T	Take a look at the next picture.
S	Er ... box.
T	A box, yes.
S	A box.
T	And what's inside the box, Pietro?
S	A box bananas.

Note the way the teacher prompts the learner to move from *box* to *a box* to *a box bananas*. *A box bananas* may not be correct, but it is clearly more grammaticized than *box*.

Learners can scaffold one another's talk, especially where they are forced to fine-tune their utterances in order to convey subtleties of meaning. We saw this happen in « p24 Chapter 2:

S1 ... the old woman beat, no hit, the young thief and and ...

S2 In the picture you can see as the old woman (**S1:** Yes) hit the young thief?

S1 Yes, I can (**S2:** I can't) see the old woman who hit the young thief. [...]

S2 But I don't see er nothing about er an old woman hitting the young thief.

Note the increasing syntactical complexity – and greater precision in meaning – as the proposition moves from *the old woman hit the young thief* (subject-verb-object) to *I don't see nothing about an old woman hitting the young thief* (subject-verb-object, the object containing a preposition phrase which in turn contains a non-finite clause!).

As speakers become more proficient, these verbal scaffolds can be gradually dismantled. It has been claimed that the vertical construction of scaffolds provides the linguistic context for grammar to emerge. As one researcher put it, 'Language learning evolves *out of* learning how to carry on conversations.'

Discovery activity

Here is another transcript of teacher-learner talk, from research carried out by Kumaravadivelu[7]. What instances of scaffolding can you find in it? (**T** = teacher; **S** = unidentified student; **S1** = an identified student; xxx indicates a missing phrase)

1	**T**	OK, that's what we're hoping to do in this class is to give you some opportunity to interact with each other and... ah... respond in an appropriate way. You know, sometimes there may be situations like Julia's car is broken and she is worried about this. She needs to she needs some help from a friend. Can you think of some other situations that might make a person worried? What situations can you think about... that might make a person worried?
2	**S**	Fire in the apartment...
3	**T**	Fire in the apartment ...*(writes on blackboard)* good...
4	**S11**	Car accident...
5	**T**	Car accident... right ...
6	**S2**	Sick...
7	**T**	Sick... in what way would you be sick?... Can you...?
8	**S**	xxx
9	**T**	You are sick... and...
10	**S**	xxx *(Ss laugh)*
11	**S2**	Sick... xxx... mind...
12	**T**	*(laughs)* Maybe a mental sickness... but... maybe you're sick and... need a doctor fast... OK. What else?
13	**S12**	Your wife... baby... xxx *(gestures)*
14	**T**	Your wife is having a baby.
15	**S**	She's having a baby xxx *(Ss laugh)*
16	**T**	Oh... yes... there's a movie called 'She's having a baby'. So what else might... ah, these are situations that might mean an emergency. What if you are just worried about something?
17	**S**	xxx future
18	**T**	Your future. OK.
19	**Ss**	xxx *(Ss laugh)*
20	**T**	Future plans.
21	**S10**	Homework...
22	**T**	Worried about your homework... All right...
23	**S**	xxx *(Ss laugh)*
24	**T**	You are worried about me?
25	**S2**	Grade... grade...
26	**T**	Oh, worried about grade... OK. That's good. Now...

Commentary ■ ■ ■

A good example of scaffolding is the sequence in turns 13 to 16, where the teacher recasts the student's non-grammaticized words and gesture (*Your wife... baby...*) into *Your wife is having a baby.* This, in turn, is modified by another student, apparently quoting the name of a film, eliciting a comment and further repetition from the teacher. There are other instances of teacher recasting (eg turns 11 and 12, turns 21 and 22, and turns 25 and 26). Notice that turns 2 and 3, and 4 and 5 involve the teacher simply echoing the learner's utterances – which, while making the utterance available to students who might not have heard it, is unlikely to provide much material for syntactic development. It's as if Mark's mother were to reply *Popped on* to Mark's *Oh popped on:* while maintaining the conversational flow, it hardly constitutes scaffolding in the strict sense of the word. However, there is another sense in which learning is scaffolded by the teacher in this extract, and that is through the provision of frames: the teacher's introduction (turn 1) establishes the purpose of the teaching sequence that is going to follow, and the final move (*That's good. Now...*) suggests a transition into a new sequence. Clear signposting of this sort lessens the likelihood of the learners 'losing the plot'. ■

Ecological grammar

The importance of scaffolding highlights the 'environmental' factors that support grammar emergence. Just as an organism needs the right conditions to grow, so too does grammar need an optimal linguistic, social and cultural 'eco-system' if it is to evolve. We may not yet know what these optimal conditions are, especially for second language acquisition, but we can be fairly sure that, just as a plant needs more than simply water, no one single factor is going to be sufficient for language growth. Input alone, or output alone, or interaction alone, are not going to do the trick. In fact, mechanistic concepts such as input and output sit uncomfortably with a more holistic, ecological view of language learning. After all, one person's input is another person's output – and each influences the other, in the same way that an organism resonates with its environment.

The educational linguist Leo van Lier argues that we should think in terms of providing not input and output opportunities as such, but *affordances:* 'An affordance is a particular property of the environment that is relevant [...] to an active perceiving organism in that environment.' A leaf, for example, affords food for one animal, shelter for another, camouflage for the third. The leaf is the same leaf, but it provides different affordances to different organisms. By analogy, classrooms should provide language affordances. 'If the language learner is active and engaged, she will perceive linguistic affordances and use them for linguistic action.' Van Lier[8] gives an example of this process at work, in describing his three-year-old son, who had grown up speaking Spanish in Peru:

> When we moved to the USA he spoke no English. He went through the classic silent period for the first few months, when he would speak no English at all, though he clearly understood a great deal. Then one day I was wheeling my cart around the local supermarket, with him sitting in the front. I had just picked up a box of Rice Krispies, when another guy came along with a cart that also had a box of Rice Krispies in it. A humorous coincidence, which Marcus noticed. At that point he produced his first English sentence: 'Look! This on this!'

Van Lier notes that the situation 'afforded' Marcus an opportunity to connect signs (Rice Krispies packets) and signifying devices (gesture and language) and audience (his father). Van Lier argues that language emergence is situated in, and stimulated by, environments which are rich in things to talk about and rich in the resources to engage with them (both verbal and non-verbal). Such was the supermarket for Marcus.

This ecological view, according to van Lier[9], assumes

> that knowledge of language for a human is like knowledge of the jungle for an animal. The animal does not 'have' the jungle; it knows how to use the jungle and to live in it. Perhaps we can say by analogy that we do not 'have' or 'possess' language, but that we learn to use it and 'live in it' [...] We 'learn' language in the same way that an animal 'learns' the forest, or a plant 'learns' the soil.

The ecological view is very suggestive. At the very least, it suggests creating classroom environments that are linguistically fertile, socially situated, interactive, and where language is available as a tool for making meaning. Moreover, it suggests that a simple input-output model of learning does not capture the full complexity of the acquisition process, and that research based on this model is of limited application.

However, we will continue to use the terms *input* and *output* in what follows – simply because they are now common currency in talking about classroom processes – at least until such terms as *affordance* become more generally accepted.

Summary

So, we have established that language learning shares features associated with other complex systems and processes. What does all this mean in terms of teaching? The (admittedly simplistic) model on page 52 suggests that, at the very least, the ingredients of language learning are a linguistic *environment*, consisting of *input* (the data stream), *output* (what emerges) and *feedback* on the output (the pressure to conform). Borrowing from the evidence of the importance of scaffolding, we should also add *interaction*. So what is new? Input, output, feedback and interaction are all elements of traditional language instruction – what used to be called *presentation, practice (+ correction)* and *production*.

Well, what the model doesn't show clearly enough perhaps, but what the theory suggests, is that:
- the input has to be massive
- items (words, phrases) have to be extracted from the input to provide the raw material for pattern formation
- the interaction needs to be meaning-driven (not simply the practice of pre-selected forms)
- the language that emerges is not predictable on the basis of the input
- the reorganization (or restructuring) of the learner's grammar is self-actualized – that is, the change agent is *in* the system, not outside it. As long as the system is open to new input the interlanguage system reorganizes itself.

So, if the system is self-organizing, what is the role of the teacher?

The teacher's role is as critical as ever, and can be summed up as consisting of these six functions:
- provider of input
- interactant

- facilitator of item learning
- facilitator of pattern detection
- provider of opportunities for output
- provider of feedback.

To which we should probably add a seventh – a function which some would argue is the most important of all:

- motivator

Where the teacher is probably *not* very effective is in the role of transmitter of grammatical facts – what used to be called grammar *presentation*. If grammar emerges and is self-organized, the teacher's attempts to force the process are likely to fall on deaf ears. It might be better to think of the teacher's role as less one of *covering* the grammar than of *uncovering* the grammar. That is, facilitating the natural processes of emergence: not forcing the grammar in, but letting the grammar *out*.

References

1 Soars, L. and Soars, J. 1993 *Headway Elementary, Teacher's Book*. Oxford: Oxford University Press
2 Oxenden et al. 1996 *English File 1, Teacher's Book*. Oxford: Oxford University Press
3 Ellis, R. 1994 *The Study of Second Language Acquisition*. Oxford: Oxford University Press
4 Gell-Mann, M. 1995 *The Quark and the Jaguar: Adventures in the simple and the complex*. London: Abacus
5 Battram, A. 1999 *Navigating Complexity*. London: The Industrial Society
6 Wells, G. 1981 *Learning through Interaction*. Cambridge: Cambridge University Press
7 Kumaravadivelu, B. 1993 'Maximising learning potential in the communicative classroom.' In *English Language Teaching Journal*, vol. 47, no. 1, pp12-21
8 van Lier, L. 2000 'The Ecology of the Language Classroom: Towards a new unity of theory, research and practice.' In *IATEFL Research SIG and Teacher Development SIG, Special Joint Issue*
9 van Lier, L. 'From Input to Affordance: Social-interactive learning from an ecological perspective.' In Lantolf, J. (ed.) 2000 *Sociocultural Theory and Second Language Learning*. Oxford: Oxford University Press

Chapter 5   Process teaching

So far we have looked at alternative approaches to grammar teaching (or better, grammar *processing*) at the level of specific task types, such as grammaticizing activities (Chapter 2) and consciousness-raising activities (Chapter 3). We have also seen (in Chapter 4) how language – and grammar in particular – follows a developmental route that shares characteristics with other complex systems, suggesting that grammar is not knowledge imported from outside but a capacity that emerges from within. In this chapter, we will look at the wider implications of a process and emergence view of grammar and see how this might affect questions of overall lesson shape, materials choice, syllabus design and even teaching style. What teaching processes, in other words, are implied by a process view of grammar?

Discovery activity

Before we look at the seven functions of the teacher outlined in the last chapter, and how they might relate to an 'uncovering' view of teaching, think about the implications for your own practice. How do you already
- provide input?
- facilitate interaction?
- facilitate item learning?
- facilitate pattern detection?
- provide output opportunities?
- provide feedback?
- motivate your learners?

How might you need to adapt your approach (if at all), consistent with an *emergence* view of language?

Commentary ■ ■ ■

Teachers I have done this task with tend to respond in one of two ways: either they don't feel that an emergence view requires any great adjustment to their present approach: 'It's what I do anyway, more or less.' Or they accept that such an approach would require a major change in their classroom practice, but that such a change would be impracticable in their present teaching context: 'It would be impossible to let grammar just emerge when you are working to a grammar-based coursebook and you have a grammar-based exam at the end of the term.' These two responses represent different forms of resistance – a normal and quite healthy reaction to the threat of change.

Occasionally there is a third view, and it goes like this: 'I'm not sure if the changes are far-reaching or practicable, but there are one or two ideas that I might just try out, partly because I am having doubts about the effectiveness of what I'm doing at the moment.'

Depending on which category you fall under, what follows may have greater or lesser relevance. Nevertheless, even the most resistant teachers have been known to experiment with a new procedure or technique from time to time. As the poet Charles Olsen wrote:

> What does not change
> is the will to change. ■

Providing input

We have already established that a lot of input seems to be necessary in order to trigger grammar emergence. The success of language immersion programmes is no doubt attributable to the fact that learners are massively exposed to the target language. This suggests that, for a start, the teacher should maximize the use of the target language in the classroom. It also suggests a powerful role for reading, especially since this can be done outside class time – indeed, may be better done outside class time, so as to allow more classroom time for activities that require more social organization, such as listening and speaking. Setting up a reading programme, whereby learners read graded readers outside class and then discuss them in class, would seem to be worthwhile. I knew a teacher whose class of advanced women students agreed to subscribe to a British women's magazine: they each received their copies through the post, and the magazine content formed the basis of all classroom work. The Internet, of course, offers enormous possibilities along these lines.

What kind of *listening* works best? Listening without understanding is unlikely to be of much benefit. As well as providing input, then, the teacher's role is to ensure that the input is intelligible. There are a whole host of ways of doing this, including:

- selecting material that the students are already familiar with, eg stories that they know well in their own language
- providing a context, eg setting the scene for a recorded listening text, providing visual support while telling a story, using video
- selecting material that is within students' linguistic competence, or adapting it accordingly
- pre-setting a task that helps focus students' attention – attention is a pre-condition for understanding
- choosing material that is intrinsically interesting – then a task is no longer necessary
- pre-teaching key vocabulary and expressions, or stopping and explaining these along the way
- repeating – providing several opportunities to listen to the text
- providing a transcript
- providing a translation
- monitoring understanding 'on-line' and mediating where necessary.

Traditional 'comprehension questions' are designed to *test* comprehension, rather than facilitate it, so they are probably not of much use except in examinations. Rather than the teacher asking comprehension questions, a better strategy might be to encourage the students to ask *comprehending* questions: 'What does X mean? What exactly did she say in the bit when...' etc.

Moreover, recorded listening texts are perhaps a less than ideal means of providing listening input, since, apart from being 'disembodied', it is impossible to adjust their content to the on-line difficulties of the learners. All you can do is stop, go back and listen again. Compare this to 'live' listening when, for example, the teacher is telling a story. Not only can the listeners interact with the speaker, but the speaker can monitor the listeners' degree of understanding and make appropriate adjustments. Moreover, the teacher's anecdote is going to be intrinsically more interesting, and therefore more motivating, than a fictitious anecdote recorded on tape. Also, if the teacher speaks naturally, the input the learners receive is likely to be more 'real' than recorded material that has been especially written for classroom purposes. This suggests that an important function of the teacher is simply *talking* to the learners. And, remember, the talk that the learners listen to doesn't have to be 100% grammatically perfect for them to infer correct patterns. The brain seems to be capable of filling in the gaps.

Discovery activity

Here is the word-for-word transcript of a story that one teacher told her class. How do you think she (a) monitored the learners' understanding, and (b) integrated this story into the lesson?

I went to a concert a few weeks ago – at the Palau de la Musica – isn't it a fabulous building? Anyway, the singer – it was a charity concert, for handicapped children, and it was very smart – the Queen's sister was there, or sister-in-law maybe. And the singer was [name], who is – well, she must be in her seventies. Do you know who she is? But she was wonderful – very erm gracious and erm gorgeous voice still. And she would sing a few songs and go off and come back on for the applause, and so on. Anyway, she was coming back on and she caught the heel of her shoe in the erm hem – you know – down here – of her dress, long skirt or something, and she went down like, like a tree, it was dreadful. In front of all these people. Everybody was [gasp]. And they helped her off stage and there was a long pause, and then she came back on again and there was this tremendous applause. And she actually sang some more songs – and of course at the end the audience went wild. But I was thinking, 'Oh how awful, and, she must have hurt herself too…'

Commentary ■ ■ ■

Here is the teacher's own account of how she monitored understanding and how she used the story.

'The story is a true one, even if not very exciting, but I think the fact that it is true helps learners understand, because their attention level is raised, they really want to understand. And I didn't read it to them, I just told it to them. That way you can watch them as you are telling them, and you can see, by the whites of their eyes, if they are understanding or not. Every now and then I checked their on-line understanding by saying things like 'OK?', 'Are you with me?' and so on. Sometimes, when I do this kind of thing, I will stop and explain any difficult vocab, write it on the board, but only if it's essential.

When I had finished, I asked them if they had any immediate questions or comments. One student asked me if I thought maybe it was a trick she did every time. Then what I often do is put them into pairs to check with each other, in their own language if necessary, more or less what they have heard. After that they usually have more questions. And I will ask questions too – questions that tell me if they have got the main outline of the story. I might also ask one of the students to tell it back in their own words. In English preferably, but in their mother tongue too, if need be. I'll do anything, in fact, to be sure that they have the right 'schema' in their heads.

What I did then was elicit a reduced version of the story back on to the board. Sometimes I get them to prepare this in pairs first. Or sometimes I record myself telling the story, so I've got the recording to refer to when we're transcribing it. Sometimes I get the students to write it on the board rather than me doing it – I might even leave the room while they're doing this, then come back and correct it. When I'm writing it up, I try to include some interesting expressions, chunks, and so on. Then I will underline these and ask the students to use as many as possible to write true sentences about themselves. In this lesson I concentrated on the adjectives – *wonderful, marvellous, dreadful* and so on, so they had to write sentences like 'A wonderful thing that happened to me...' etc. They then show their sentences to each other in groups of three and they ask questions about each other's sentences: this way you get a little discussion going. They then write a short report about their group's discussion.' ∎

Facilitating interaction

According to the principle of scaffolding, the teacher can provide the student with the necessary language support to coax out more complex language. This is different from *eliciting*: the objective behind eliciting is to get the student to produce an item (a word or a structure) that the teacher has pre-selected. The focus is entirely on producing the right forms, as in this example from Nunan[1]:

T Clothes. Clothes.

S *(inaudible)*

T What's the question? *(inaudible)* Not colour. What's the question for clothes, you ask – the question – for clothes? What... ? The question. Come on, we did this last week. Can you remember? The question?

S What clothes do you like?

S What kind of clothes do you like?

T Not like.

S Wear.

T Wear, yeah. What's the question? Wear.

S What kind of a...

S What ...

S Where do you buy...

T Wear. No, not where do you buy. Clothes.

S What clothes do you usually wear?

T Good question – what clothes do you usually wear? What about now – what? What's the question now what...?

Because the teacher's agenda is a specific form (*What are you wearing?*) this kind of interaction is a far remove from the scaffolded interaction between parents and children, where the focus is simply on the joint construction of meaning. In eliciting there is no natural language emergence: it's more like getting blood out of a stone. Compare this example:

T Hi.

S Hi. I'm new. This class.

T You're new. OK. What's your name?

S Barbara.

T Barbara. Were you a transfer from another class, Barbara? Or...

S Yes, from *(indistinct name)*, Mr (...)

T Right. So, you are... you're studying the book? Have you got the book?

S   Yes, but I don't have the book.

T   You haven't got the book yet. OK. Well maybe, if you can sit next to Neus, you can share the book…

Notice that in this case the teacher's questions are *real*. That is to say, the teacher doesn't know the answer to the questions (*What's your name?*) whereas in the earlier extract all the teacher's questions were *display* questions, ie they were questions designed so that the learners could display their knowledge (*What's the question for clothes?*). (A teacher trainer colleague makes it a rule that teachers should 'tell what they know and ask only what they don't'.)

Notice also how the teacher in the second extract *repeats* and *recasts* (ie correctly reformulates) the student's talk:

S   Hi. I'm new. This class.

T   You're new.

    […]

S   I don't have the book.

T   You haven't got the book yet.

This is exactly what Mark's mother is doing (page 53) when she says: 'Oh yes. The fire popped on, didn't it?'

The use of real questions coupled with repetitions and recasts are a feature of scaffolded talk. Most teachers do this instinctively, especially when they are chatting with their learners before or after the lesson. What many teachers don't realize is that this kind of interaction is an ideal site for language emergence – for uncovering the rudimentary grammar that the learners already have, and for shaping and extending it into something nearer the target. In Chapter 3 we saw how this works in exchanges such as the following:

≪ pp 33–4

T   What did you do at the weekend, Ana?

S   I go to the mountains.

T   *Last* weekend, I mean.

S   Last weekend, I… erm… *went* to the mountains.

T   Did you go alone?

S   No, I go with my friend.

T   You *went* with your friend?

S   Yes, I went with my friend. ■

Discovery activity

Here is a transcript of a segment of classroom talk, part of some research carried out by Steve Walsh[2]. Identify the ways that the teacher supports and shapes one student's (S4) story:

1 **S4**   the good news is my sister who live in Korea send eh…

2 **T**   SENT

3 **S4**   sent credit card to me

4 **T**   ooh very good news

5 **S4**   but bad news is

6 **T**   the bad news is

7 **S4**   I don't know password…

8	**Ss**	password/password
9	**S1**	pin number
10	**T**	pin number
11	**S4**	what?
12	**T**	pin number pin number
13	**Ss**	ah pin number/pen number
14	**T**	pin PIN not pen pin
15	**Ss**	pin/pin number/p-i-n
16	**S1**	I always forgot my pin number
17	**S**	ah pin number
18	**T**	I don't know my pin number
19	**S5**	she can phone you on mobile phone
20	**T**	she can...
21	**S5**	he can say you
22	**T**	she can...
23	**S5**	she can tell your pin number
24	**T**	yeah she can tell you your pin number
25	**S5**	she can tell you this pin number by phone
26	**S4**	but I can't eh ring her because eh because eh the time eh
27	**T**	the time difference?
28	**S4**	time difference

Commentary ■ ■ ■

The teacher's interventions seem to have five main functions:
1 correcting (eg turns 2 and 6)
2 prompting, that is, inviting a self-correction (turns 20 and 22)
3 recasting (turns 18 and 24)
4 supplying needed language (turns 10 and 27)
5 commenting (turn 4)

The net effect of these interventions is to maintain a conversational flow while at the same time to embed learning opportunities in the talk. Notice that it is not just the teacher who contributes to the 'scaffolding' process – other students are involved too (eg turns 9, 15 and 19). ■

This kind of chat or small talk typically happens *outside* the lesson, or on the fringes of the lesson. If it has the learning potential that some researchers claim, we should try to maximize it and incorporate it into the lesson proper.

There are two basic principles worth following:
- Seek to increase the chances of small talk occurring, by, for example, asking learners to personalize the lesson material, creating a relaxed and informal classroom atmosphere, setting an example by talking about yourself.
- Exploit small talk incidents when they do occur, by, for example, drawing out students when they say something 'real', by responding to *what* learners are saying, not just the way they are saying it, and by not being afraid to abandon the lesson plan in order to mine an interesting seam of talk.

Facilitating item learning

It may seem out of place to be talking about the acquisition of words, and of word-like units (or chunks), in a book about grammar. But, apart from supplying the need for a serviceable vocabulary, word acquisition is a prerequisite for the development of grammar. This seems to be the case whether you take the cognitivist view, that unanalysed chunks (such as *gimme*, *I'm gonna...*) are available for subsequent analysis into their components (*give me*, *I'm going to...*) or whether you take a connectionist view. Connectionism claims, remember, that rule-like behaviour (grammar) emerges out of the strengthening of connections between initially isolated, but gradually associated, items (eg words). These associations are formed because the words in question share one or more characteristics. For example, they may all be nouns that are never found in conjunction with the indefinite article *a/an*: *salt, water, information, furniture*, etc. Or they are adjectives that do not collocate with *very*: *excellent, famished, unique, hilarious*, etc. Or they are words like *must, can, should*, etc that are followed by a bare infinitive (*come, have, work*, etc). Or they are verb + *up* combinations: *pay up, use up, finish up, drink up*, etc.

According to this view, the learner needs a critical mass of encounters with such items before they start to cohere and fuse into generative patterns. Such a view argues for maximizing the quantity of words and chunks the learner both meets and stores in memory.

Memory! That's the key. Any activity that helps learners memorize new words is going to be worth doing. And the more the merrier. Two of the most effective ways of memorizing vocabulary are the *keyword technique* and the use of *word cards*. Both activities are described by Nation[3].

Keyword technique

In this technique the learners create an unusual association between the word form and its meaning. Let us imagine that an Indonesian learner of English wants to remember the meaning of the English word *parrot*. First the learner thinks of an Indonesian word that sounds like *parrot* or like a part of *parrot* – for example, the Indonesian word *parit*, which means 'a ditch'. This is the keyword. Second, the learner imagines a parrot lying in a ditch! The more striking and unusual the image, the more effective it is.

Word cards

Each word form and its translation should be put on a small card with the foreign word form on one side and the translation on the other. This is much more efficient than setting the words out in lists in a book or on a sheet of paper. First, learners can look at the foreign word and make an effort to recall its translation without seeing the translation. It helps learning to say the foreign word while trying to think of its translation. Second, the learners can rearrange the cards so that they are not using the sequence of words in the list to help recall. Third, they can put the words which give them the most difficulty at the beginning of their pile of cards so that they can give them extra attention. Piles of these cards are easily carried around, and they can be studied whenever learners have a free moment.

Learners need training in each of these techniques, and so the teacher should set time aside at the beginning of a course to do this. The teacher should demonstrate the keyword technique, using a few examples of his or her own. (But, remember, the best memory devices are the ones the learners come up with themselves.) It also helps if, initially, the teacher provides learners with pieces of card (about the size of a business card) to start making their own collection. Then, whenever new vocabulary comes up in class, eg out of a text, the learners should be given time in the lesson to make keyword associations and prepare their word cards. They do this individually, but it helps if they regularly share their associations and test each other using their sets of cards.

Here, for example, are the words that one student selected for her word cards from the teacher's story text on page 60:

handicapped / in her seventies / gorgeous / applause / heel / hem / dreadful

Facilitating pattern detection

If the learner's grammar is self-organizing and emergent, as claimed, does the teacher have any role at all in the process of pattern detection? Certainly, the traditional 'chalk-and-talk' role, with the teacher at the board explaining finer points of grammar, seems not only to have no long-term positive effect on grammar development, but takes time away from where it could more usefully be directed – at *using* the language. Nevertheless, even if teachers can exert little direct influence on grammar emergence, they can probably nudge the learners in the right direction. Systems theorists, while recognizing the principle of self-organization, acknowledge that some external 'leverage' of the environment may help to make change in one direction more likely than change in another.

« pp35–6

« pp36–40

One way of applying leverage to the learning environment is through *noticing* tasks. In Chapter 3 we argued that noticing is a prerequisite for learning, and that attention is a prerequisite for noticing. The teacher is well positioned to maximize attention and direct noticing. The activities designed to promote noticing (outlined in Chapter 3) are more likely to trigger restructuring than if the teacher simply explained the rules, it was argued, because they make the grammar *matter*. In order for restructuring to take place, the learner must either want or need to go that extra mile.

« pp40–41

Wanting to move closer in the direction of the target language may be socially motivated – and we will deal with that later. *Needing* to be more precise may be motivated by communicative necessity: there comes a point where baby talk simply doesn't convey the delicacy of meaning required. Grammar interpretation tasks are a good way of alerting learners to these finer shades of meaning encoded through grammar.

But, in the end, it's the learners who have to do the noticing: as we said in the last chapter, you can lead Hamdi to the grammar, but you can't make him notice it. The teacher's role may be more a training one: training the learners to become good noticers, that is good 'language detectives'. To do this, the teacher needs to be good at pattern detection, too.

One way of doing this is simply to *pull out* (by commenting on, or underlining, or otherwise highlighting) recurrent or salient patterns in a text.

What constitutes a pattern, though? A pattern is any regularity that has productive potential, ie that can act as a template for the creation of novel utterances. The pattern *pay up, use up, finish up, drink up*, etc produces *eat up* and *end up*. The pattern *must do, will do, can do*, etc generalizes to *should do* and *may do*. The pattern *some salt, some information, some furniture* extends to *some fruit juice, some advice* and *some soap*. Notice that patterns in language cut across the traditional boundaries between vocabulary and grammar. In fact, there are patterns everywhere: all we need to do is look for them.

Another important feature of patterning is that words that share patterns also tend to share meanings. So the addition of the word *up* to verbs such as *pay, use, finish, drink, eat* and *end* adds the sense of 'to completion': *The government finally paid up; Drink up: it's closing time!* The verbs *must, will, can, should* and *may* share meanings of 'likelihood, possibility': *That must be Ted; It should be a nice day tomorrow; I may be late.* And singular nouns that follow *some* have an unbounded, fluid sort of meaning: *There's too much salt in this soup; I'm overloaded with information; There was fruit juice all over the floor...*

Discovery activity

In the following groups of phrases and sentences, identify the 'odd one out' – ie the one that doesn't fit into the pattern. Then decide what common meaning the other four items in each set share:

A 1 the baby's bottle
2 the nation's struggle
3 the teacher's sick
4 the nurse's pay
5 the government's defeat

B 1 The plane was hi-jacked by a woman.
2 The tourists were attacked by a gang.
3 The soldier was hit by a bullet.
4 The trains collided by a river.
5 Three hundred people were killed by the earthquake.

C 1 I'm not used to the noise yet.
2 They used to work in a circus.
3 Didn't there use to be a shop there?
4 I never used to smoke.
5 It didn't use to be so dirty.

D 1 The ship sank.
2 A door opened.
3 Lots of people drowned.
4 A dog barked.
5 My glasses broke.

Commentary ■ ■ ■

A: In phrase 3 (*the teacher's sick*) the apostrophe represents a contracted verb (*is*), whereas in the others the apostrophe indicates possession. The meaning that the other phrases have in common is that the second noun *belongs to* or *pertains to* the first noun.

B: Sentence 4 doesn't fit. Sentences 1, 2, 3 and 5 are passive and *by* indicates the agent. Sentence 4 is active, and *by* indicates where the action took place.

C: Sentence 1 is the odd one out: in the others *use(d) to* indicates a finished state or habit in the past, whereas *I'm not used to* has the meaning *I haven't got accustomed to...*

D: This is more difficult. The odd one out is 4. The verbs in the other sentences are of a special type that can be used both intransitively (without an object) or transitively (with an object). Thus: *The ship sank* or *Something sank the ship.* Similarly, *A door opened / Somebody opened a door.* But you can't *bark a dog.* Verbs like *open, sink, break, drown* are called ergative verbs. Ergative verbs tend to express *transition,* either in the form of *changing states* or of *movement.* When used intransitively (as in the examples above) they do not attribute the change to any particular agent. They can be used, therefore, to avoid apportioning blame or responsibility. *My glasses broke* but I'm not saying who broke them[4]. ■

Patterns not only cut across the boundaries of grammar and vocabulary – they can ripple through whole texts. Any instance of a repetition may be a clue to a pattern. Here, for example, is a letter I picked out of the newspaper I just happened to be reading:

> Peter Webster (March 23) says that Australia does not have an 'underclass', and that is why it has not got a crack cocaine problem. But what about our huge heroin problem? Not only does Australia have an underclass, but it has possibly one of the worst heroin problems in the world (which is not restricted to the underclass). There are many reasons for drug use, but those most commonly used are there not because of underclasses but because of more mundane reasons, such as supply.
>
> Sophie Masson,
> Invergowrie, NSW,
> Australia

Notice how certain words ripple through the text (these have been circled).

> (1) Peter Webster (March 23) says that (Australia) does not have an ('underclass'), and that is why it has not got a crack cocaine (problem). (2) But what about our huge (heroin) (problem)? (3) Not only does (Australia) have an (underclass) but it has possibly one of the worst (heroin) (problems) in the world (which is not restricted to the (underclass). (4) There are many (reasons) for drug (use), but those most commonly (used) are there not because of (underclasses) but because of more mundane (reasons), such as supply.
>
> Sophie Masson,
>
> Invergowrie, NSW,
>
> (Australia)

Notice, too, how constructions in one sentence are echoed in other constructions in the text. These 'echoes' can be schematized like this:

(1) | Australia (not) have underclass | + | (not) have drug problem |

(3) (Not) | Australia (not) have underclass | + | (not) have drug problem |

Sentence 3 both echoes and contradicts sentence 1 and uses the pattern *not only... but...* to do this: 'Not only does Australia have... but it has...'

There is also a chain of cause and effect running through the text:

| Australia not have drug problem | *because* | Australia not have underclass |

| Australia have drug problem | *not because* | Australia not have underclass |

| Australia have drug problem | *because* | supply |

Notice how cause and effect is encoded in the grammar and lexis:

> *...and that is why...*

There are many reasons...
not because of... but because of...
... more mundane reasons...

The key word in the whole text is probably *not*. It appears five times:

Australia does *not* have...
it has *not* got...
Not only does Australia have...
not restricted to the underclass...
not because of underclasses...

But is also frequent (four instances):

But what about...
not only... *but...*
but those most commonly used...
not because... *but* because...

The frequency of *not* and *but* suggests that the overall message of the text is one of denial and contradiction. To prepare students to write texts with a similar function, all of these patterns would be worth highlighting.

And we haven't even looked at the overall patterning of the argument of the text:

Claim (*Peter Webster says...*)
Challenge (*But what about...?*)
Contradiction (*Not only does... but...*)
Counterclaim (*There are many reasons... but... such as...*)

By comparing this text with other, similar texts that set out to do the same thing (such as leader articles in newspapers, party political broadcasts, etc) we will probably find that these same elements co-occur, and maybe even in the same order. This, too, constitutes a pattern. Thus, any one text is likely to be patterned at the level of individual words, of grammar and of overall organization (or discourse).

Discovery activity

Here is another text. Before looking at what one teacher did with it, look for some patterns that would be worth highlighting:

Dolphins help mute boy to speak

Dolphins have enabled an eight-year-old boy to speak for the first time.

Starved of oxygen at birth, Nikki Brice, from Somerset, England, has always had the physical ability to speak, but he has never learned to use it. Speech therapists tried to teach him to speak, but with no success. So the boy's family raised £10,500 and took him to the Human Dolphin Therapy Centre in Miami, Florida. Within days of being at the centre, where youngsters swim with the mammals, he had uttered his first few halting words.

Therapists are now training Nikki to exercise his vocal cords and, day by day, he is picking up new words.

Scientists are still undecided as to why dolphins have a healing effect on people with learning difficulties. Some believe the underwater sounds that dolphins make may play a part.

Commentary ■ ■ ■

The patterns the teacher chose to highlight were the ways the idea of ability was encoded in the pattern: *help someone to do something*.

What the teacher did first was to check that students had got the gist of the passage: they chose a summary that best matched the text and then discussed their response to the text – what did they think it was about dolphins that helped him to speak? Is it true that dolphins can communicate? etc.

She then drew their attention to the headline: *Dolphins help mute boy to speak* and asked them to see if they could find other examples of the pattern *V + n + to-inf* (that is, a verb followed by a noun followed by the infinitive with *to*). This is what they came up with:

Dolphins <u>help mute boy to speak</u>
Dolphins <u>have enabled an eight-year-old boy to speak</u>
Speech therapists tried to <u>teach him to speak</u>
Therapists are now <u>training Nikki to exercise</u>

Having established that the verbs *help*, *enable*, *teach* and *train* all take this pattern, and all have the common meaning of *enabling*, the teacher added the following verbs to the list:

stimulate
motivate
inspire
influence

(Note that the teacher chose this particular pattern to focus on because not only does it recur in the text but it represents the *core meaning* of the text – not surprisingly it has been chosen to summarize the text in the form of the headline. Reducing a text to its core meanings often helps identify its key lexical and grammatical patterns.)

Having done that, she asked them to tell their partner about something that they couldn't do once and that they were helped (or taught, trained, inspired, etc) to do. She told them this example from her own experience:

Watching French videos and going to French language films helped me to understand French better. And understanding French motivated me to continue studying.

Finally, she used their personal anecdotes as the basis for an open class chat, in which they contributed their experiences and commented on each others'. ■

What we have been doing, then, is using *input* (in the form of texts) as sources of *intake* – the 'taking in' of language data that may serve to trigger the reorganization of the learner's grammar. To do this we have been exploiting what might be called the *outpull* of texts – the patterns and regularities that can be 'pulled out' of them. The teacher is strategically placed to mediate between texts and learners, converting input into intake through classroom processes of outpull.

Providing output opportunities

Ask any group of students what they most want out of their language class and chances are they will say *speaking practice* or *conversation* or something else along these lines. Traditionally, such opportunities had to be balanced against the need to provide learners with the *facts* of the language in the form of grammar rules. Because grammar explanations tend to expand to fill the time available for them, output opportunities were often severely limited.

But (as was argued in Chapter 4) an emergent-grammar view of learning suggests that explaining the grammar (or 'covering the grammar') is of limited value. Better let the learners talk, and then *uncover* the grammar. Besides, the talk that is generated provides useful *text* which, in turn, can be used as a source of input for both item learning and pattern detection. This means that somehow the learner talk needs to be 'captured'. That is, it is not enough simply to get the students talking. Their talk needs to be pinned down and made available for some kind of scrutiny or analysis.

The following activities are ways of both generating learner output and then capturing it to use as input.

Model text

Tell the class a personal story/opinion/facts related to the topic of the lesson (eg clothes, travel, football). (At this stage, you could ask learners to write a résumé of this, while you do the same on the board or an overhead projector transparency, for comparison purposes.) Then the students create their own texts, based on your 'model', and tell these to their classmates in pairs. In order to capture the language, the classmates write a summary of what they have been told. The teacher monitors, corrects and extracts any interesting language features worth commenting on.

Student story

Interview one of the students about the lesson topic, eg their knowledge/experience/ attitudes about clothes, football, music, etc. The others listen and then write up the interview, including questions. (The student who has been interviewed does the same.) The teacher monitors and helps. Then they interview each other and report back to the class.

CLL (Community Language Learning)

Students sit in a circle and record a 'conversation' about the topic, taking turns to speak. Before each utterance is recorded, it is rehearsed for approval. The teacher acts solely as consultant, supplying vocabulary and expressions as needed, but does not attempt to direct the course of the conversation – neither the content nor the turn-taking. Utterance by utterance the conversation is built up. Then the entire conversation is played back and written up on the board. Language points that emerge are highlighted and commented on.

Paper conversation

« Chapter 2 p26 This is like on-line chat: students write their conversation (on the topic) in pairs/groups, passing a sheet of paper back and forth. This helps slow up their language processing, allowing time to attend to form. It also allows you to monitor and correct.

Teacher interview

The teacher establishes a topic, eg my last summer holiday, my eating habits, etc, and students prepare questions about this on slips of paper, working in groups. They submit each question as soon as they have written it and the teacher writes a response, correcting the question if necessary, and returning it. Once the groups have sufficient questions, they then use the answers to write a summary, which is then exchanged and read by other groups.

Free discussion

Generate an open class chat about the theme of the lesson or the text that you have been using. You can prepare students for this by writing up a few questions for them to think about silently and/or discuss with their partner, before opening it out. Draw students out, and keep the focus off heavy correction. If/Once the discussion gets going let it run. Then put the students into pairs or threes to write a summary of what was said, eg as if reporting on the class for an absent class member. Monitor and correct. Deal with any interesting language features that emerge.

How about trying out one of these activities in a class of your own?

Providing feedback

« pp48–50 We saw in Chapter 4 that complex systems require feedback from their environment if they are to adapt and evolve. Similarly, in the language learning environment, learners require feedback. Simply providing input opportunities and output opportunities is probably not enough for restructuring to take place.

» pp33–40 In Chapter 3 we looked at ways of providing feedback on form through the use of both overt and covert correction techniques embedded in conversational exchanges. Another type of feedback loop is provided by those activities where learners are encouraged to make comparisons between their output and those of a more proficient speaker (or writer) of the language.

One such technique (and one which has been around for a long time) is called *retranslation*. Essentially it involves the following steps:

1 Students (working individually or in pairs) translate a short text into their own language. The translation should sound as natural and idiomatic as possible.
2 Then (after a lapse of time – say, in the next lesson) they retranslate the mother tongue text back into English. This is done without seeing the original (English) text.
3 They then compare their retranslation with the original text. This comparison stage is the feedback: they can see how near or far they were from the original – in other words, they are 'noticing the gap'.

Here is an example, using the following original text, which was adapted from *Who's Who in the Twentieth Century*[5].

Los Angeles, Victoria de (1923 -)

Spanish soprano. Born in Barcelona into a musical family, she soon learnt to sing and play the guitar. She went on to study at the Barcelona Conservatory, where she made her recital debut in 1944. Her professional opera debut came the following year at the Teatro del Liceo. After winning an international singing contest in Geneva in 1947 she became widely known. In 1950 she made her US debut, as well as her first appearance in Britain. She sings a wide variety of operatic roles, as well as Spanish folk songs. In recitals she sometimes accompanies herself on the guitar.

Here is the retranslation (from English to Spanish and back to English) done by one student:

Victoria de Los Angeles; Spanish soprano

Born in Barcelona in a music family she soon learnt to sing and play guitar. She went on study in Conservatori of Barcelona, where she made her debut in 1944. Her opera debut went on next year in the Teatro del Liceo. After winning an international song contest in Geneve in 1947 she was widely recognized. In 1950 she made her debut in US as well as her first appearance in Britain. She sings a wide opera roles as well as folks Spanish songs. In recitals sometimes she accompanied herself with a guitar.

When the learner compared his text with the original, he noticed – and asked the teacher about – the use of the definite article *the* with *guitar* in phrases like *plays the guitar*. He also corrected the mixed up noun phrase *folks Spanish songs* but needed to have his misuse of *went on (Her opera debut went on…)* pointed out to him.

Another long-established 'gap-noticing' activity is known variously as dicto-comp, dictogloss, or grammar dictation. The basic procedure is:
1 Learners listen to a short text once, maybe twice, in its entirety.
2 They then reconstruct it from memory, either individually or in pairs or groups.
3 The reconstructed text is then compared with the original.

Unlike a traditional dictation, the learners don't hear the text phrase by phrase or line by line, but in its entirety. This means they can't memorize it verbatim. They simply retain the gist of the text and then have to 'grammar it up', using their available resources. In the comparison stage, they can see how near or far they were from the original.

Here is how one group of students reconstructed the following text, which was read once to them at normal speed:

There was a young woman of Riga
Who went for a ride on a tiger.
They returned from the ride
With the woman inside
And a smile on the face of the tiger.

One student, working alone, produced the following:

There was a woman from Riga who were on a tiger to make a ride. When they come back the woman was in tiger and the tiger were smiling.

Working with two other students they then came up with this version:

There was a young woman from Riga who go for ride on a tiger. The tiger come back with the woman inside and a smile on the tiger.

Finally, the class (of nine students) working altogether produced this text:

There was a young woman of Riga who went for a ride on a tiger. The tiger returned with the woman inside and a smile on its face.

Notice how the collaborative work of grammaring has produced a grammatically correct text, even though it lacks some of the stylistic features of the original – which, at this stage, the students were then shown.

Feedback, then, need not come solely from the teacher: learners can access their own feedback through text comparison activities such as retranslation and dictogloss. Feedback becomes part of an input–output cycle:

text   →   student's reconstruction   →   comparison

input   **output**   **feedback**

In a recent experimental study which explored the effects of text reconstruction and comparison cycles, one student commented, 'It was excellent because you became conscious which are your mistakes. When I saw a model, I noticed exactly what and where are my mistakes.'

Finally, here is one more activity that incorporates a cycle of output and feedback. This comes from Earl Stevick's book *Success with Foreign Languages*[6]:

> Another of my favourite techniques is to tell something to a speaker of the language and have that person tell the same thing back to me in correct, natural form. I then tell the same thing again, bearing in mind the way in which I have just heard it [ie having noticed the gap]. This cycle can repeat itself two or three times... An essential feature of this technique is that the text we are swapping back and forth originates with me, so that I control the content and do not have to worry about generating non-verbal images to match what is in someone else's mind.

Motivating your learners

What motivates grammaring? What makes learners want to restructure, to push themselves, to climb new grammatical heights? Why do some learners grammar up while others bottom out? And what does this have to do with their overall motivation as learners?

In natural learning contexts, ie children learning their first language, or new arrivals to a country picking up a second language, the learners are generally highly motivated by the need to become a member of the local speech community. (Remember Andrea in « pp18–19 Chapter 2 – the Italian living in London who seemed to be more keen to integrate than his compatriot Santo?) Such learners will be sensitive to feedback that signals how near or how far they are from this target. Positive feedback in this kind of situation might take the form of laughter at a joke well told, or having someone say 'Why, I could have sworn you were a local!' Negative feedback, on the other hand, would be when the person you are talking to conspicuously changes register and starts to talk to you in a form of pidgin, as if you were from the planet Mars.

In classrooms, the social pressure to conform is less acute. Everyone, after all, is in the same boat, and the teacher is usually a lot more tolerant of the tell-tale signs of foreignness, like a strong accent, inappropriate use of slang, or muddled idioms (such as a student of mine who wrote 'I don't want to blow my own horn but...').

So, what motivates classroom learners to keep moving their language towards the target variety, if it is not social factors? The answer is probably *communicative effectiveness* – the need to fine-tune forms in order to express exactly the meaning required. This is why feedback is so important: without feedback the learner might never realize that his or her output was ambiguous or less than fully intelligible. This, or course, means positive as well as negative feedback. Positive feedback acknowledges that the learner's utterance was communicatively successful, even if it wasn't entirely accurate:

S I go to the club.
T Oh, great. Well, have fun.

As Rod Ellis once put it, 'It is the need to get meanings across and the pleasure experienced when this is achieved that motivates second language acquisition.'

But this assumes that the meanings the student is expressing are important enough to want to get right. This is seldom the case in traditional grammar practice activities, such as drills. Learners have very little, if any, personal investment in the kind of meanings typically found in exercises such as the following:

> *Make sentences about Jack, using the prompts below.*
>
> *For example:*
> *never/prison*
>
> *He has never been to prison.*
>
> *1   never/Brazil*
> *2   never/raw fish*
> *3   never/married*
> *4   never/Rolls Royce*
> *5   never/lottery*

Personalising lesson content so that it is relevant to the learner is obviously a major factor in terms of upping the meaningfulness of activities. Compare the exercise just quoted with the following:

> *What is the best/worst thing you have never done?*
>
> *Write sentences, using this model:*
>
> I have never won the lottery.
>
> *Put your sentences in two columns: BEST, WORST*

The adjustment is slight, but the spin off in terms of learner investment is likely to be significant.

Discovery activity

Here is a typical coursebook exercise. How could you adapt it to make it more relevant to (and hence more engaging for) the learners?

Student A

Here is your diary for the week. Talk to Student B. You have to arrange a time to meet when you are both free.

Monday		Thursday	
morning	driving lesson	morning	
afternoon		afternoon	Jill's wedding
evening	Spanish class	evening	cinema
Tuesday		**Friday**	
morning	dentist	morning	hairdresser
afternoon	tennis	afternoon	
evening	dinner with sister	evening	
Wednesday			
morning			
afternoon	shopping		
evening			

Student B

Here is your diary for the week. Talk to Student A. You have to arrange a time to meet when you are both free.

Monday		Thursday	
morning		morning	gym
afternoon	meeting with accountant	afternoon	
evening	Bob's Birthday party	evening	French lesson
Tuesday		**Friday**	
morning	work	morning	
afternoon	work	afternoon	
evening		evening	theatre
Wednesday			
morning	doctor		
afternoon			
evening	babysitting		

Commentary ■ ■ ■

One rather obvious but productive way of personalizing this task is simply to let students fill in some blank diary pages with their own real or imagined plans for the forthcoming few days and then to try and arrange a meeting. The neat symmetry of the coursebook materials will be lost, and they may 'solve' the task much sooner, but the possibilities for developing the talk, based on their own plans, may ultimately be more productive and more memorable. ■

But there is little point in personalizing classroom activities if the teacher's feedback fails to acknowledge the learner's investment. It is easy, in the cut-and-thrust of classroom interactions, to overlook, or simply not hear, the fact that learners are attempting to express meanings that are important to them. But not being listened to can be extremely demotivating – just as it is in real life when your partner, your children, or your colleagues at work (inadvertently) ignore you. Or, almost as bad, when they concentrate not on what you are saying but only on how you are saying it. The following exchange is invented, but it is not untypical of teacher–student interactions when the agenda of the former is focused exclusively on *form*:

T Has anyone ever had an accident?
S Yes, me. I breaked my leg.
T Broke.
S Broke. I broke my leg in three places.
T Good.

To summarize, then, these are what I consider the optimal conditions for motivation:
- a balance of positive and negative feedback
- communicative success
- relevance and investment
- being listened to

Finally, it is worth pointing out that, even for students who lack a motive for learning English (ie they have no immediate need for it), motivation is still possible, if the above conditions are met. Motivation comes from a sense of being valued. As Finocchiaro put it[7]:

> Motivation is the feeling nurtured primarily by the classroom teacher in the learning situation. The moment of truth – the enhancement of motivation – occurs when the teacher closes the classroom door, greets his (or her) students with a warm, welcoming smile, and proceeds to interact with various individuals by making comments or asking questions which indicate personal concern.

Changing your style

By now I hope it's clear that an emergent pedagogy – one in which grammar is not covered but *uncovered* – is one which is characterized by the following features:
- the teacher talks to learners (but not only that...)
- the learners talk to the teacher (but not only that...)
- the teacher listens to the learners (but not only that...)
- the teacher and learners interact (but not only that...)
- the content of the lesson is largely based on the interaction between teacher and learners, and between learners and each other.

This is a radically different pedagogy from the one identified at the beginning of this chapter and characterized as 'transmission' style. Transmission style teachers, if you remember, deliver the grammar in the form of pre-selected and pre-packaged items: *I revised the second and third conditionals and* would *and* should...Typically, when teachers talk about this kind of teaching, they use transitive verbs (*I taught the grammar*) of which the teacher is the agent (*I...*). The object of the verb is typically grammar-as-thing (*I taught the present perfect*) or the students (*I taught them*) or both (*I taught them the present perfect*).

What would an emergent conception of teaching be like? Maybe it would be one that was described in terms of object-less verbs, in which the students, as much as the teacher, were the agents, and in which processes were mental as much as material:

The students talked and listened and understood.
They thought, reflected and remembered.
They concentrated and worked.
Topics came up. Problems arose.
Language emerged and the grammar developed.

In fact, such descriptions of teaching do exist. The visionary New Zealand school teacher, Sylvia Ashton-Warner[8], writing in 1963, described her primary classroom in terms that are consistent with an emergent view of language development. Rather than 'teaching' pre-selected words, the children were invited to ask her for 'key words' – words that were important to them individually – which she wrote on to cards and which they then taught each other and wove in to their own stories:

> Each afternoon... the words, whether known or not, are rubbed from the board and each morning the new ones go up. It's exciting for us all. No one ever knows what's coming. Wonderful words appear... This is the main reading of the day. They master their own story first, then tackle someone else's. There is opportunity to read out their own story and it is from this reading that discussions arise.

Note the 'back-seat' role of the teacher in this description: not a single sentence has the teacher as agent. Note, also, the use of intransitive verbs to indicate emergent processes: *New [words] go up ... No one ever knows what's coming... discussions arise.*

Discovery activity

Here is another extract from Ashton-Warner's book *Teacher*[8]. What other evidence can you find that suggests her approach is a far remove from transmission-style teaching?

> I am continuing experiments at school on the words of most vital meaning to a child to begin with. These words seem to be sorting themselves out with alarming clarity around the two main instincts: fear and sex.
>
> I began to suspect this when I tried the word 'kiss.' The children, five-year-old Maoris, discussed it excitedly. They returned to the book to find the place once more and the next morning ran in early to tell us that they could still spell 'kiss'.
>
> I took the hint and looked for a word to represent the first and strongest instinct, fear. But the only one I had was 'frightened,' which did not recommend itself as a first word on account of its length. Although I knew that it has always been an easy word to teach, and one that I have used extensively. However, I tried it, and it won, even against 'kiss', which is according to the importance of the two instincts. It was learnt immediately by the new entrants, and another thing occurred that I had not noticed before. An intelligent, new Maori, just five, repeated the word 'frightened' over and over again to himself.
>
> 'Cried' was third.
>
> In 'frightened' and 'cried' I feel that I have the two words for that side of nature, fear, representing cause and effect. Now, with 'kiss' established I think there must be another word, stronger than 'kiss,' representing the cause on this side.

It may be 'love'.

But I seldom hear them use 'love'. And have not tested it for that reason. I mean to test this word on Monday.

Commentary ■ ■ ■

This teacher's non-transmissive style is captured in the way she approaches teaching in an experimental, investigative and intensely curious manner. Rather than being imposed, the content of her teaching emerges from her research and in response to feedback from the children. The children, in fact, are the unwitting shapers of the curriculum. The teacher's use of intransitive verbs and her foregrounding of the children as sentence subjects is another indication of a non-transmissive style:

These words seem to be <u>sorting themselves out</u>...
Another thing <u>occurred</u>...
<u>The children</u>... discussed it excitedly.
<u>They</u> returned to the book...

Where the teacher is agent, she is typically the agent of cognitive verbs, suggesting her role is not so much do-er as thinker and reflector:

I began to <u>suspect</u> this...
I <u>took the hint</u>...
I <u>feel</u> that I have the two words...
I <u>think</u> there must be another word...
I <u>mean</u> to test this...

■

A compromise?

A presentation-transmission approach to teaching grammar assumes that there is something the learners don't know, and that the teacher's role is to provide them with that knowledge. It is a *deficit* model of learning. An emergent view of grammar, on the other hand, starts from the assumption that there is something the learners can already do, and that the teacher's role is to help them to do it more effectively. It could therefore be described as an *empowering* model of learning.

An emergent view of grammar has the following implications:
- Work from texts and topics rather than from a structural syllabus.
- Generate language and then look for items and patterns.
- Talk to the learners and scaffold their emergent language.

But will all the grammar be covered – or even uncovered? – you may be wondering. I believe it will. The assumption is that, *if* a fairly wide range of topics are chosen, and *if* a fairly representative range of texts are used, and *if* there is ongoing work on item learning and pattern detection, and *if* the input–output–feedback cycle is in constant motion, and *if* the classroom dynamic is intrinsically motivating, then all the grammar that the learners will ever need will emerge in time. This is a big assumption, with a lot of *ifs*. Nevertheless, traditional grammar teaching is also based on some fairly sweeping assumptions – number one being that *if* the teacher teaches something, the learner learns it. Generations of frustrated language learners (as well as many frustrated language teachers) know better.

However, a more cautious approach, one which incorporates the traditional grammar syllabus, may *just* be compatible with an emergent view of grammar. After all, the 'noticing' activities outlined in Chapter 3 can easily be slotted into the practice stage of the traditional presentation–practice model of instruction. And most, if not all, of the activities described in this chapter are compatible with a syllabus of pre-selected grammar items.

Imagine, for example, it's Tuesday and the syllabus says 'Teach them phrasal verbs!' The teacher, instead of *presenting* nine phrasal verbs representative of three different patterns, simply dictates nine statements about herself and the learners have to write them down and decide if they are true or not. For example:

1 On Saturday evenings I usually go out.
2 I often borrow things and forget to give them back.
3 Whenever I feel bored I phone up a friend.
4 If it's a nice day, I often head for the beach.
5 On Sunday mornings I always sleep in.
6 I always put some music on when I get home.
7 I don't like cooking so I tend to eat out.
8 If I'm feeling lazy, I'll phone for a pizza.
9 I look after my neighbours' cat when they're away.

Students are free to ask questions, either to clarify the meaning of the sentences, or to elicit further information in order to do the task. The teacher then tells them the 'answers', commenting on the different situations (*It's not true: in fact I get up early on Sundays and drive to my friends' place in the country*). At this stage, the students can be asked to find the phrasal verbs and to group them into three patterns:

- Verb + adverb (1, 5, 7)
- Verb + noun + adverb (or verb + adverb + noun) (2, 3, 6)
- Verb + preposition + noun (4, 8, 9)

The teacher elicits – or supplies – further examples of phrasal verbs for each pattern. The students then make true/false sentences about themselves, choosing from the verbs. They exchange these sentences, guess, discuss and report.

So, what is new? Not much – except that the productive, personalized nature of the task may have spin-off in areas of language that have nothing to do with the 'grammar of the day', but may be more in tune with the learners' developing, emergent grammar. For example, they may pick up on these different ways of talking about habits and routines:

On ... evenings/mornings, I usually/always ...
I often ... and ...
Whenever I ..., I ...
If ..., I often ...
I (always) ... when ...
I don't like ... so I tend to ...
If ..., I'll ...

Or items or expressions may emerge from the joint discussions and may be 'captured' in the report stage.

In other words, there may be ways of satisfying both the *external* syllabus and the *internal* one within the same lesson. This (weaker) version of an emergent approach would have, as its basic principles, the following:

- *if* working from a structural syllabus, exploit the texts and topics associated with it in order to...
- generate language and then look for items and patterns
- talk to the learners and scaffold their emergent language

This watered-down version of an emergent approach accepts the grammar syllabus as a fact of life, but uses it as a pretext to introduce language-rich tasks that reach parts that the impoverished grammar syllabus does not. In the end, it boils down to a question of weighting: should you give more weight to teaching or to learning? If the latter, then time spent covering the grammar should not be at the expense of time spent uncovering it.

Finally, the difference between covering grammar and uncovering it may have less to do with the type of syllabus or the design of lessons or the choice of materials than with the teacher's own attitudes, values and beliefs. In other words, grammaring is less a method than a state of mind. States of mind, too, are complex, emergent and resistant to external leverage. But small effects – like butterflies – can precipitate major changes. It is our hope that this book may have triggered, if not a storm, at least a little turbulence in your state of mind.

References

1 Nunan, D. 'The language teacher as decision maker.' In Brindley, G. (ed.) 1990 *The Second Language Curriculum in Action.* Sydney: National Centre for English Language Teaching and Research

2 Walsh, S. 2000 (unpublished thesis) 'Construction or Osbtruction: Teacher talk and learner involvement in the EFL classroom.'

3 Nation, I.S.P. 1990 *Teaching and Learning Vocabulary.* Boston MA: Heinle and Heinle

4 Two useful references to help sensitize you to the way English is patterned are:
Collins COBUILD Grammar Patterns : 1 Verbs 1996 London: HarperCollins
Collins COBUILD Grammar Patterns : 2 Nouns and Adjectives 1998 London: HarperCollins

5 Briggs, A. 1999 *Who's Who in the Twentieth Century.* Aylesbury: Market House Books Ltd

6 Stevick, E. 1989 *Success with Foreign Languages.* Hemel Hempstead: Prentice Hall

7 Finocchiaro, M. 'Motivation: its crucial role in language learning.' In Hines, M. and Rutherford, W. (eds.) 1981 *On TESOL '81.* New York: TESOL (quoted in Ellis, R. 1994 *The Study of Second Language Acquisition.* Oxford: Oxford University Press)

8 Ashton-Warner, S. 1963, 1980 *Teacher.* London: Virago

Photocopiable materials

In the following pages you will find materials that have been designed to realize the aims of a *process* approach to teaching grammar. Some of the tasks target specific *discrete items* of grammar (such as the present perfect, reported speech, the passive, etc) while others require students to engage with a number of grammatical items at once.

These tasks have been divided into three chapters, matching the three more practical chapters of the book – Chapters 2, 3 and 5:
*   Chapter 6: Grammaring tasks – that is, recognition and production tasks in which grammar is 'added' (see Chapter 2)
*   Chapter 7: Consciousness-raising tasks – including 'noticing' and 'grammar interpretation' tasks (see Chapter 3)
*   Chapter 8: Grammar emergence tasks – including reformulation and reconstruction tasks (see Chapter 5)

Chapter 6   **Grammaring tasks**

In Chapter 1, we saw how language moves from a lexical to a more grammatical mode in order to cope with the demands imposed by distance. This distance can be of at least three kinds:
*   contextual distance – especially of space and time
*   conceptual distance – eg when talking about hypothetical meaning
*   social distance – eg between strangers, or where there is power inequality

If all communication was about real things happening here and now, and occurred between familiar social equals, we could probably get by using 'telegramese': 'Nice day. Coffee? Busy? The kids?' etc. However, since a lot of communication does not meet these 'zero-distance' conditions, learners need to learn how to deploy grammatical forms in order to bridge the context and/or concept and/or social gaps. The activities in this section attempt to help students to do that.

Grammaring: Task Sheet 1 (p82)   Expanding headlines

Grammaring: Task Sheet 2 (p83)   Ambiguous headlines

These first two task sheets require students to 'add grammar' to de-grammared, essentially lexical, texts. The natural follow-on to any of these exercises is to ask the students to write their own headlines and to exchange and 'unpack' them.

Grammaring: Task Sheet 1

1 Here are some newspaper headlines. Expand them so as to summarize the story.

For example: | **BANKS WARN HOMEOWNERS: INTEREST RATES TO RISE**

Banks have warned homeowners that interest rates will rise.
Or *Banks are warning homeowners that interest rates are going to rise.*

1 BUS STRIKE TALKS CALLED OFF

2 FREE EYE TESTS OFFERED TO ALL OVER-65s

3 SHARK ATTACK VICTIM BACK AT SCHOOL

4 LOG TRUCK CRASH DRIVER NOT GUILTY

5 DOLPHINS HELP MUTE BOY SPEAK

6 GOVERNMENT PROMISES NEW MONEY FOR HEALTH SERVICE

7 CRACK DOWN ON SPENDING, SCHOOLS TOLD

2 Compare your expanded headlines or summaries with other students. Are they the same? If not, do the differences make a difference in meaning?
For example:
Banks have warned homeowners... / Banks are warning homeowners...
There is a difference in meaning here. In the first sentence, the warning was made at some indefinite time in the recent past; in the second, the warning is still being made.
...interest rates will rise. / ... interest rates are going to rise.
There is no significant difference in meaning here.

3 Now, write headlines for these stories. How short can you make them, without losing the sense of the story?
1 The government has announced plans to cut spending on the military.
2 The captain of a tanker involved in an oil spill off the French coast has been found guilty of negligence.
3 Parties involved in the stalled peace talks in Biombo have agreed to resume their discussions.
4 An unidentified man, who fooled bank staff into thinking the banana he was carrying under his jacket was a gun, held up a city bank this morning and made off with over $15,000.

4 Write a headline that summarizes something interesting or unusual that happened to you recently. For example:

BROTHER'S WEDDING A BIG SUCCESS

DRIVING TEST UPSET

Show it to your classmates – tell them your story and ask them about theirs.

Grammaring: *Task Sheet 2*

1 Each of these headlines has two meanings: the intended one and an unintended one. Can you expand them to show these two meanings more clearly?

| JOHNSON TEACHER TALKS VERY SLOW |

| N.J. JUDGE TO RULE ON NUDE BEACH |

| MAN HELD IN FIRE AT HIS PSYCHOTHERAPIST'S HOME |

| GARDEN GROVE RESIDENT NAIVE, FOOLISH JUDGE SAYS |

| POLICE DISCOVER CRACK IN AUSTRALIA |

| COMPLAINTS ABOUT NBA REFEREES GROWING UGLY |

| REAGAN WINS ON BUDGET, BUT MORE LIES AHEAD |

| KICKING BABY CONSIDERED TO BE HEALTHY |

| SISTERS REUNITED AFTER 18 YEARS IN CHECKOUT LINE AT SUPERMARKET |

2 Choose one of the headlines and write a short news item, based on its *unintended* meaning. For example:

COMPLAINTS ABOUT NBA REFEREES GROWING UGLY

The National Basketball Association (NBA) admitted yesterday that complaints about the ugliness of their referees are on the increase. Television companies are particularly incensed by the growing ugliness of referees. A CBS spokesman said 'Referees used to be quite handsome, but now they are pig ugly. Our viewers are switching to other channels when the basketball comes on.' An NBA spokeswoman said that selection of referees is under review, and that approaches are being made to Hollywood with a view to recruiting more attractive refs.

Photocopiable

Grammaring: Task Sheet 3 (p85) Expanding messages

This task focuses on the context gap involved in conveying messages from one party to another party by means of a third. The greater the gap, the more grammar needs to be enlisted – both in terms of syntax (ie word order) and the use of pronouns.

Answers

1   The answer is 4. The situation is this: Dave phones Luke and leaves a message on Luke's answerphone. The message is for Luke's flatmate, Pam. Luke writes the message down.
2   1   'Hi, Jack, this is Jill here. How about meeting at the club tomorrow? Don't forget your tennis racquet.'
    2   'Hi, Bernard. Stéphane here. I need Birget's phone number. Do you think you could phone me this evening?'
    3   'Hi, Sam. It's Oliver here. Look, I don't have Nancy's phone number. Could you possibly phone her and ask her if she could phone me tomorrow morning?'

Grammaring: Task Sheet 4 (pp86–7) Grammaring game

This is a board game designed to develop students' ability to grammaticize language using minimal means. The sentences produced in the game should, ideally, be written up and discussed by the class, the teacher challenging the students to put them into a context, and, if the class is a monolingual one, translate them into their mother tongue.

Give students the following instructions, either verbally, or photocopy them.

Materials needed: one counter for each student and one dice for each pair of students

Object of the game

The object of the game is to produce the most number of grammatically well-formed sentences (of four words or more) within a time limit, eg 15 minutes.
- Work together in pairs, taking turns to throw the dice.
- One of the pair moves their counter around the board marked GRAMMAR and the other round the board marked WORDS.
- Pairs 'collect' **words** and **grammatical items** by landing on a square. When you land on a square, write down the word on a piece of paper.
- When you have collected enough items to make a sentence, write it down. Sentences should be correctly formed and have of a minimum of four words.
- You can only use verb tenses for which you have collected the appropriate ending (*-ed*, *-ing*, etc). You may have to make adjustments for spelling (eg 'study' + '-ed' = *studied*).
- You cannot reuse words or items already assembled into sentences.
- Continue collecting words and forming sentences until the time is up. The pair with the most correct sentences wins. In the event of a tie, the pair with fewest unused words or items is the winner.

Grammaring: Task Sheet 3

1 Here is a written message someone left after listening to their answerphone. What was the original answerphone message?:

1 'Hi, this is Dave. Can you ask Pam to phone me tonight at home and give him your passport number?'

2 'Hi, this is Dave. Can you ask Pam to phone him tonight at home and give her my passport number?'

3 'Hi, this is Dave. Can you ask Pam to phone Luke tonight at home and give him your passport number?'

4 'Hi, this is Dave. Can you ask Pam to phone me tonight at home and give me her passport number?'

5 'Hi, this is Dave. Can you ask Pam to phone him tonight at home and give me her passport number?'

6 'Hi, this is Luke. Can you ask Pam to phone Dave tonight and give me her passport number?'

Pam:
message from Dave –
needs your passport
number – phone him
tonight at home.
Thanks,
Luke.

2 Now, write the answerphone messages for these written messages:

1
Jack.
Jill phoned
Wants to meet
you at the club
tomorrow. Bring
your tennis
racquet.
Ta, Ellen.

2
Bernard.
Stéphane phoned.
Needs Birget's
phone number.
Phone him this
evening.
Cheers, Jacob.

3
Sam,
Oliver phoned.
Hasn't got Nancy's
number. Phone
her to tell her to
phone
him tomorrow
morning.
See you, Todd.

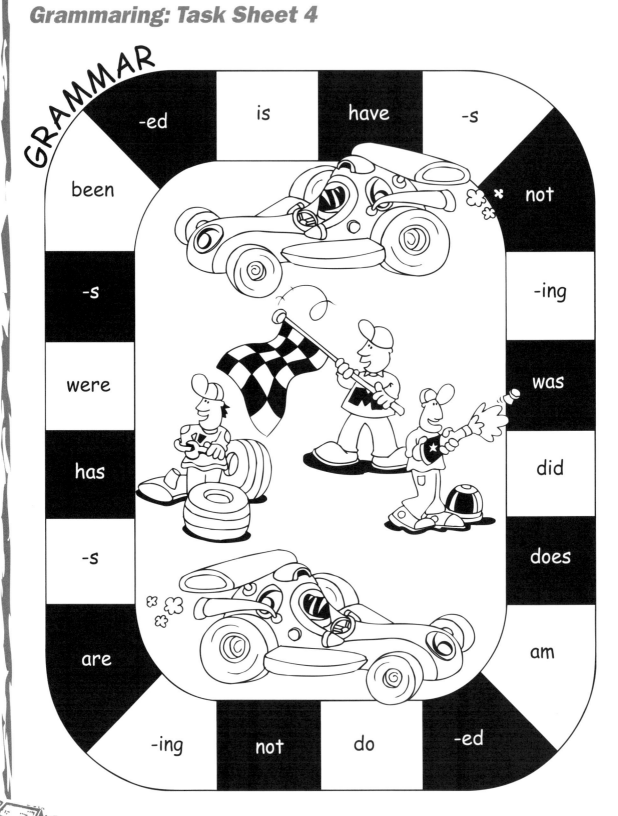

GRAMMAR

-ed   is   have   -s

been   not

-s   -ing

were   was

has   did

-s   does

are   am

-ing   not   do   -ed

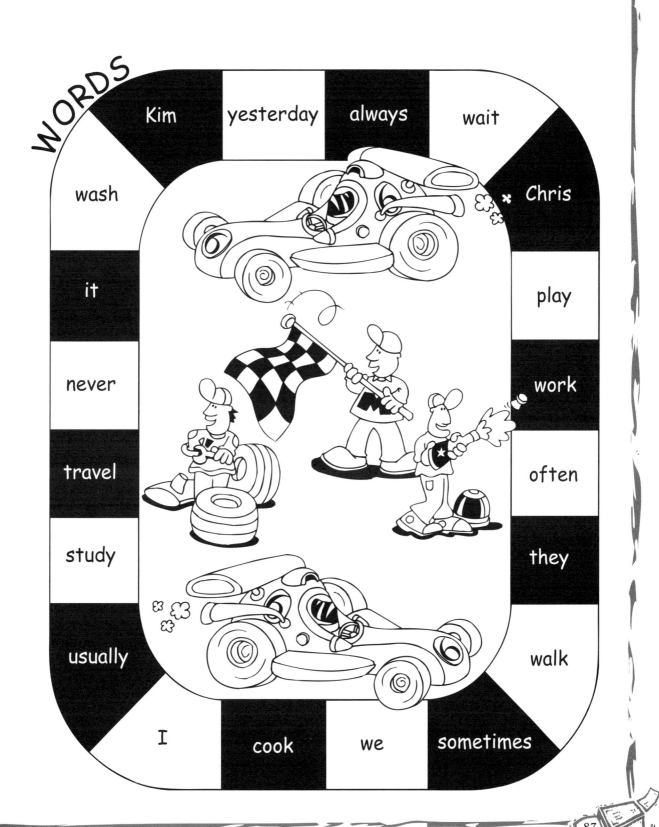

WORDS

Kim | yesterday | always | wait
wash | | | Chris
it | | | play
never | | | work
travel | | | often
study | | | they
usually | | | walk
I | cook | we | sometimes

Grammaring: Task Sheet 5 (p89) Physical distance

This task is designed to raise students' awareness as to the effect of distance on grammar. All languages have linguistic means to indicate the vantage point – both spatial and temporal – of the speaker in relation to what the speaker is talking about. While in some languages the system is quite complicated, in English there is a simple two-way distinction: *here + now* versus *there + then*. Linguistic ways of signalling here-ness versus there-ness and now-ness versus then-ness are called *deictic* devices. These devices are particularly important when we are reporting what someone says. Traditional rules for reported speech suggest that when reporting, you use 'backshift' – ie you move everything one tense 'back'. But this is an oversimplistic account of the rules and doesn't take into account context factors, such as the *time* and *place* of the reporting. This task is designed to sensitize students to the importance of these context factors and the way they influence grammaring processes.

Before you begin, check that students are familiar with how 'ago' becomes 'previously' when talking about events that finished in the past. 'Before' could be used as an alternative to 'previously'.

Answers

1 1 b)   2 c)   3 d)   4 a)

2 1 'My ship was wrecked here twenty years ago.'
    a) He said his ship was wrecked here 20 years ago.
    b) He said his ship was wrecked there 20 years ago.
    c) He said his ship had been wrecked here 20 years previously/before.
    d) He said his ship had been wrecked there 20 years previously/before.

  2 'I don't know what this island is called.'
    a) He said he doesn't know what this island is called.
    b) He said he doesn't know what that island is called.
    c) He said he didn't know what this island was called.
    d) He said he didn't know what that island was called.

  3 'I had a friend here but he died ten years ago.'
    a) He said he had a friend here but he died ten years ago.
    b) He said he had a friend there but he died ten years ago.
    c) He said he had had a friend here but he had died ten years previously/before.
    d) He said he had had a friend there but he had died ten years previously/before.

Grammaring: Task Sheet 5

1 **Match the speech bubble with the picture.**

2 **Now, write four different 'reports' – one for each of the situations above – for the following statements made by the old man:**

1 'My ship was wrecked here twenty years ago.'
2 'I don't know what this island is called.'
3 'I had a friend here but he died ten years ago.'

Grammaring: Task Sheet 6 (p91) Social distance

This task looks at the effect of social distance on language. Social distance is affected by **rank** (ie is there a difference in status between the speakers?) and **familiarity**. As a general rule, the more social distance, the more grammaring is involved.

Answers

1   Features of the second dialogue that make it more formal are:
- little or no ellipsis, ie leaving out words, as in *(Have you) Got any small change?*
- fully syntactic sentences, similar to written language
- complex sentence structure, with subordinate clauses, including conditional clauses, eg *if that's no trouble / if that's possible*
- frequent use of modal verbs: *would, might, will*
- less colloquial vocabulary, eg *certainly* rather that *sure*; *thank you* rather than *ta*.

Context factors that might cause such a high degree of formality include:
- relationship of speakers, eg lack of familiarity (social distance)
- formality of the situation, eg business meeting, not college canteen
- performance factors – speakers may be conscious of being overheard, therefore on their best 'linguistic behaviour'.

Grammaring: Task Sheet 6

1 **Compare these two dialogues. What features of the second dialogue make it more formal than the first? What differences in the speakers or situation would explain this?**

Dialogue 1

Anyone fancy a coffee?

Sure, if you're getting one.

Got any small change?

Here.

Ta. Tomorrow it's on me.

No worries.

Milk? Sugar?

Black, two sugars.

Something to eat?

Get us a chocolate bar, will you?

OK. Back in a sec.

Dialogue 2

Would anyone like a hot drink?

Well, I wouldn't mind a coffee, if it's no trouble.

Not at all. You wouldn't happen to have a fifty pence coin, would you?

I think I just might. Here you are.

Thank you. I'll pay you back.

Please, I wouldn't hear of it.

Would you like milk and sugar?

I'll have it black, with two spoonfuls of sugar, if that's possible.

Can I get you something to eat?

Well, a chocolate bar would be nice, if they have any.

Certainly. I'll be back shortly.

2 **Change this informal dialogue into a more formal one. In what kinds of situation would each one be appropriate?**

Come in and have a seat.

Do you smoke?

So, you want a job here?

OK, let's see your papers.

Can you start today?

OK. Just sign here.

That's OK. Shut the door
   on the way out.

Thanks.

No, thanks.

Yes.

Here.

Not tomorrow?

Thanks.

3 **Write an informal dialogue based on one of the following situations. Make it clear who is speaking to who. Exchange it with a partner and rewrite the dialogue more formally. What differences in the context (speakers/situation) might have caused the differences in the language?**

- asking someone for the loan of some money
- inviting someone for a meal
- asking about someone's health
- preparing a party

Photocopiable

Grammaring: Task Sheet 7 (p93) Hypothetical distance

As well as physical and social distance, grammar allows us to express hypothetical distance – that is, the distance between the here-and-now world and the world of imagination and dreams. Typically, hypothetical meaning is expressed using conditional structures. These three activities focus on how these structures are used to express hypothetical distance, both at the time of speaking and in the past.

Answers

1   1 d)   2 c)   3 a)   4 b)

2   The errors here mainly relate to hypothetical distance:

I imagined I will have a wonderful time. = I imagined I would have a wonderful time.

Maybe it will be the best holiday of my life. = Maybe it would be the best holiday of my life.

But if I knew what a terrible experience it was I never went there. = But if I had known what a terrible experience it was going to be, I would never have gone there.

You should advise me before I travel not to pack such value things. = You should have advised me before I travelled not to pack such valuable things.

If I know that I will carry them with me in the plane. = If I had known that, I would have carried them on the plane with me.

I bring my own towel if I knew. = I would have brought my own towel if I had known.

If we know this, we did not book this holiday. = If we had known this, we would not have booked this holiday.

... if you tell me the correct informations I took more money with me. = ... if you had given me the correct information, I would have taken more money with me.

If I think this was happen I taked a bus. = If I had thought this would happen I would have taken a bus.

It would be faster. = It would have been faster.

If you are an honour company you will pay me back my money... = If you are/were an honourable company you will/would pay me back my money...

Only you know that I wish I never choice this terrible holiday and I never travel with you in the future. = I only want you to know that I wish I had never chosen this terrible holiday and I will never travel with you in the future.

Grammaring: Task Sheet 7

1 **Which person is talking? Match the speech bubble with the picture.**

2 **Read this letter written by an angry holidaymaker to a tour company. It contains a number of errors. Can you correct them?**

Dear Sirs,

I am writing to complain about the terrible holiday I had, thanks to your company. As you may remember, I travelled to Sicily last summer on a package tour. I imagined I will have a wonderful time. Maybe it will be the best holiday of my life. But if I knew what a terrible experience it was I never went there. The first thing was that all my luggage was lost and when it arrived at last things had been taken from it. I lost an expensive camera and a leather jacket. You should advise me before I travel not to pack such value things. If I know that I will carry them with me in the plane.

The next problem was that our hotel did not provide any towels! I bring my own towel if I knew. And nobody told us that the hotel is a long way from the beach. As an old person I cannot walk a long way. If we know this, we did not book this holiday. Also the hotel was more expensive than we expected, because we had to pay for drinks and meals. I didn't have enough money but if you tell me the correct informations I took more money with me.

Finally, worst of all, the return flight was delayed for two days and we had to wait in the airport. If I think this was happen I taked a bus. It would be faster. If you are an honour company you will pay me back my money but I don't expect this. Only you know that I wish I never choice this terrible holiday and I never travel with you in the future.

Yours sincerely,

R. Petoniz

3 **What sort of person are you? How helpful are you? Make four lists:**

Things I do   Things I would do if...
Things I have done   Things I would have done if...

Compare your lists with other students. Do the same for the following questions:

How brave are you?   How generous are you?   How impulsive are you?

Grammaring: Task Sheet 8 (p95) Propositional clusters

These exercises aim at developing students' sensitivity to the way grammar interacts with text, especially with regard to the choices between active and passive, and the use of cleft sentences (*It was the frog that kissed the princess…*).

Answers

2 1 b)   2 d)   3 a)   4 c)   Note that in examples 1 and 3, the choice is determined by the need to maintain topic consistency from one sentence to the next. Examples 2 and 4 use the cleft construction to give special prominence to a contrasting proposition.

3 Possible contexts might be:

1 When the King and Queen arrived at the school the King made a speech. The Queen was given flowers by the children. They were then shown the new gymnasium…

2 The entire school turned out to greet the royal couple. The children gave the Queen flowers. The teachers performed a traditional dance…

3 The newspaper said that the teachers gave the Queen flowers. But this was not true. It was the children that gave the Queen flowers. The teachers presented her with a book.

4 The King is not liked. At a recent school visit this was obvious. It was the Queen who was given flowers by the children. The King was ignored completely.

Grammaring: Task Sheet 9 (p96) Passives

This grammaticization task demonstrates how discourse considerations can determine grammatical form. The active-passive distinction is not arbitrary: the passive has the important function of making the topic of the text the subject of the sentence – even if it is the object of the verb!

Answers

1 1 b)   2 a)   3 b)   4 a)   5 b)   6 b)
2 1 It was painted by Picasso in 1937.
    2 He invented the electric light in 1879.
    3 It was invented by Wallace Carrothers in 1935.
    4 It was discovered by Abel Tasman in 1642.
    5 Tati directed *Mr Hulot's Holiday* in 1953.

Grammaring: Task Sheet 10 (p97) Text reconstruction

This requires students to add the grammar to a lexical base. This time the task is done at the text level. You can also adapt texts of your own choosing for this kind of task.

Grammaring: Task Sheet 11 (p98) Grammar-less poems

Poetry, especially modern poetry, is often pared down to a largely lexical core. This task compares poetry and prose and encourages students to activate grammaring processes in order to convert one to the other.

Grammaring: Task Sheet 12 (p99) Schema-bending

This task is a schema-bending one: it focuses on the grammar processes needed to rearrange the schema of a text so that it no longer follows either the chronological order of events or the reader's expectations.

Grammaring: Task Sheet 8

1 How many sentences can you make with the following elements, in any order, adding grammatical words only (eg articles, prepositions, auxiliaries, relative pronouns, etc)?

> Kim   dog   cure   vet

2 Which of the following sentences fits best into each of the 'mini-contexts' below? That is, which sentence fits into the missing sentence slot?

1 Kim's dog was cured by the vet.
2 It was the vet that cured Kim's dog.
3 The vet cured Kim's dog.
4 It was Kim's dog that was cured by the vet.

a) Kim has two neighbours: a doctor and a vet.
....
The doctor took out Kim's appendix.

b) Two of Kim's pets were ill last week.
....
His hamster recovered by itself.

c) I was wrong in thinking that Jane's cat had been cured.
....
Jane's cat is still sick.

d) For years Kim thought that his father had cured his dog.
....
His father simply took it to the clinic.

3 Now write short contexts for these sentences:

1 The Queen was given flowers by the children.
2 The children gave the Queen flowers.
3 It was the children that gave the Queen flowers.
4 It was the Queen who was given flowers by the children.

Grammaring: Task Sheet 9

1 Look at this short text:

The Curies worked together in Paris. They discovered radium in 1898.

The subject of the first sentence (*The Curies*) is the subject of the second sentence (*They*).

Now, complete these two-sentence texts by choosing the best sentence to follow.

1 Radium is a radioactive substance.
   a) The Curies discovered it in 1898.
   b) It was discovered by the Curies in 1898.

2 Albert Einstein was a Swiss physicist.
   a) He developed the Theory of Relativity.
   b) The Theory of Relativity was developed by him.

3 Joseph Salk was an American microbiologist.
   a) The first polio vaccine was produced by him.
   b) He produced the first polio vaccine.

4 Pluto is the ninth planet of the solar system.
   a) It was discovered in 1930 by Clyde Tombaugh.
   b) Clyde Tombaugh discovered it in 1930.

5 *Gone With The Wind* won several Oscars.
   a) Victor Fleming directed it.
   b) It was directed by Victor Fleming.

6 Agatha Christie was a writer of detective fiction.
   a) *Death on the Nile* was written by her.
   b) She wrote *Death on the Nile*.

2 Use the word prompts to write a second sentence to complete these short texts. You may need to change the order of the words.

1 *Guernica* portrays the horror of war.
   Picasso / paint / 1937

2 Edison was one of the world's greatest inventors.
   electric light / invent / 1879

3 Nylon is a synthetic textile.
   Wallace Carrothers / invent / 1935

4 Tasmania is an island in southern Australia.
   Abel Tasman / discover / 1642

5 Jacques Tati was a French film director.
   Tati / direct / *Mr Hulot's Holiday* / 1953

Grammaring: Task Sheet 10

1 Expand this headline into a full sentence. Can you predict the story?

> ## MAN PROPOSES IN AIRPORT, WOMAN ACCEPTS ON PLANE

2 Now, use the notes (in the order given) to write a newspaper text of six sentences. You may need to change the form of some of the words.

when Charles Devlin propose Lilian Lyle outside duty-free shop Rome airport she tell
have wait reply
not have wait long
mid-flight Heathrow Captain Murray Smiles announce over airliner address system
'have message Charles Devlin
proposal marriage Lilian accept'
passengers applaud cabin crew offer congratulations Ahmed Habibi passenger Dubai
emerge first-class cabin bear two gold watch offer couple
declare most romantic thing hear 30 years

3 Compare your text with the original story at the bottom of the page.

4 Now, see if you can make a one-sentence news item out of the following notes:

birdwatcher protest fishermen Newhaven Sussex they bare backsides shout abuse
he look through binoculars town pier later discover they mistake he fisheries
inspector

fold here   *fold here*

- -

Exercise 3   **Here is the original text:**

When Charles Devlin proposed to Lilian Lyle outside the duty-free shop at Rome airport, she told him that he would have to wait for a reply.

He did not have to wait long. In mid-flight to Heathrow, Captain Murray Smiles announced over the airliner's address system: 'I have a message for Charles Devlin. His proposal of marriage to Lilian has been accepted.'

Passengers applauded, cabin crew offered congratulations and Ahmed Habibi, a passenger from Dubai, emerged from the first-class cabin bearing two gold watches that he offered to the couple. It was, he declared, the most romantic thing he had heard for 30 years.

Exercise 4
Here is the original news item:

A BIRDWATCHER who protested to fishermen at Newhaven, Sussex, after they bared their backsides and shouted abuse at him while he looked through binoculars from the town pier, later discovered they mistook him for a fisheries inspector.

97

Photocopiable

Grammaring: Task Sheet 11

1 **Read this description (A). Compare it with the poem (B). What are the differences?**

A

I am sitting on the sand and watching the sea. The sun is setting. There is a fisherman pulling his boat out of the water and up the beach, and there are birds flying and screaming, fighting for pieces of fish. There is an old man walking his dog along the beach, throwing sticks for it to catch. Now I can hear someone singing, far away. Now I can hear nothing, apart from the sound of the waves quietly breaking on the shore.

B

sitting on the sand

watching the sea

                        the sun setting

a fisherman pulling his boat

                    out of the water

birds flying, screaming, fighting

                    for pieces of fish

an old man walking his dog

                throwing sticks

someone singing, far away

then nothing

only the sound of waves

                  quietly breaking

2 **Change this description into a poem:**

We were walking in the mountains. There was a strong wind blowing and above us dark clouds were forming. It was late. There was no sign of the little house. Then suddenly, we saw the moon rising over the mountain. We could see the path leading to the house. There was a light burning in the window. We were home at last!

3 **Now, change this poem into a prose description:**

parting at dawn

clouds turning from red to gold

a light rain falling

somewhere a dog is barking

and the car stands humming

your hand in mine

eyes not meeting

only two hearts beating

the night too short

and too long

the day that is coming

Ruth Norby

Grammaring: Task Sheet 12

1 **Look at this news item. Then number the events below in the order that they actually happened.**

WRESTLING MATCH ON JUMBO JET

Passengers wrestled a drunk Burmese to the floor as he tried to pull the pilot of a Cathay Pacific jumbo jet out of his seat minutes before landing. One business-class passenger was injured in the melée.

The Burmese passenger, who was not named, entered the cockpit and grabbed the British

pilot after staggering upstairs with a bottle of whiskey, pushing aside three flight crew on the way.

Three business class passengers leapt in to help. One passenger broke a wrist in the scuffle. But they succeeded in freeing the pilot, who then landed the plane safely.

The passenger had started drinking as soon as the plane took off from Singapore, one crew member said. He was arrested shortly after landing in Bangkok.

The co-pilot had been in full control of the plane throughout the incident, an airline spokeswoman said.

Events

Passengers wrestled a drunk man to the floor. ☐

The drunk man tried to pull the pilot out of his seat. ☐

A passenger was injured in the melée. ☐

The drunk man entered the cockpit. ☐

He grabbed the pilot. ☐

He staggered upstairs with a bottle of whiskey. ☐

He pushed three flight crew out of the way. ☐

Three business class passengers leapt in to help. ☐

One passenger broke his wrist. ☐

They succeeded in freeing the pilot. ☐

The pilot landed the plane safely. ☐

The passenger started drinking. ☐

The plane took off from Singapore. ☐

He was arrested. ☐

2 **Now, without looking at the original story, look at the list of events and rewrite them to reconstruct the original story.**

3 **Here are the events of a news story in the order they happened. Write the story, beginning with the sentence: 'A woman nearly died yesterday...'**

1 A man went to Costa Rica on business.
2 He bought a carpet for his wife.
3 He returned.
4 He gave the carpet to his wife.
5 A spider was inside it.
6 His wife was bitten by the spider.
7 She nearly died.
8 The spider was caught.
9 The woman was taken to hospital.
10 She was treated and she recovered.
11 The spider is being examined by experts.
12 The carpet has been cleaned.

Photocopiable

Chapter 7   **Consciousness-raising tasks**

The set of consciousness-raising tasks is designed to raise learners' awareness regarding specific grammatical items in order to promote the 'restructuring' of their mental grammar. In Chapter 3 it was argued that understanding (or 'interpreting') grammar choices is a prerequisite for this restructuring process: learners need to see not only that there are specific meanings associated with specific forms, but that the meaning differences between similar forms really matter. In other words, there is a big difference between saying: 'Waiter, there's chicken in this salad' and 'Waiter, there's a chicken in this salad'. It is understanding these differences that is the point of 'grammar interpretation tasks'. The following tasks, then, aim to force the learners to notice important grammar distinctions. They do not cover all areas of problematic grammar, of course, but they may provide the teacher with a blueprint for producing similar tasks for other grammar items.

Consciousness-raising: Task Sheet 1 (p101)
Modals – grammar interpretation task

This task focuses on modal verbs that express obligation (*you have to...*), permission and freedom from obligation (*you can... /you don't have to...*), prohibition (*you can't...*) and desirability (*you should/shouldn't...*). Students commonly confuse these forms and meanings, interpreting *you don't have to...* as *you can't...* or *you mustn't...* , for example. The exercise appears to focus on the facts – whether the voting age is 18, for example, when in actual fact the key to the exercise is in the choice of modal verb: it is not the case that *you have to* vote when you are 18, but that *you can*. It pays, therefore, to let the students do the exercise in pairs or small groups and then go over the first three or four answers in class. They may then need a chance to revise their answers, again in pairs, to take into account the importance of modal meaning in answering the questions.

Activity 4 is designed to encourage the free-flow of opinions, while at the same time forcing some attention on to the use of the modal verbs. Students can modify the statements either by adding conditions (eg ... *except in the case of...*) or by changing the modal verb. (Depending on the age, sensitivity or cultural background of your students, you may want to omit or adapt some statements).

Answers

1   1   False. You can vote when you are 18.
     2   False. You can't marry until you are 16.
     3   False. You have to pay for a seat on trains once you turn 5.
     4   True.
     5   True.
     6   True.
     7   True.
     8   False. You have to have a licence.
     9   True.
    10   True.

Consciousness-raising: Task Sheet 1

1 Are these sentences true or false?

In Britain...

1 ... you have to vote when you are 18.
2 ... you don't have to marry until you are 16.
3 ... you should pay for a seat on trains once you turn 5.
4 ... you don't have to do military service.
5 ... you can buy cigarettes once you turn 16.
6 ... you shouldn't smoke.
7 ... you can't buy a pet yourself until you are 12.
8 ... you can drive when you are 17, but you should have a licence.
9 ... you should see a dentist regularly.
10 ... you have to start your education by the time you are 5.

2 Now, correct the false sentences so that they are true.

....

....

....

....

....

....

3 Write a similar true/false quiz for your own country.

4 The government is considering introducing some new laws. In groups, read and discuss each proposal. Change each statement in any way you like, so that it reflects the opinion of everyone in the group.

1 Young people should pay rent to their parents.
2 The Internet must be censored.
3 Children don't have to be educated in schools.
4 Famous people have to be protected from the media.
5 Sports people shouldn't make money from advertising.
6 The government can tap telephone calls.
7 Everyone except children has to pay taxes.
8 Politicians can accept gifts but not money.
9 Smokers have to pay for their own health care.
10 Minority languages don't have to be protected.
11 Same-sex couples can marry but they can't adopt children.
12 People have to get a permit to own a gun.
13 Capital punishment can be used for some crimes.
14 Parents with more than two children can get assistance from the government.
15 People with terminal illnesses don't have to stay alive if they don't want to.
16 Private business has to support culture and the arts.

101
Photocopiable

Consciousness-raising: Task Sheet 2 (p103)
Articles – grammar interpretation task

This interpretation task contrasts countability and uncountability in nouns as signalled by the use of an article (*a/an*) and the so-called 'zero article', ie the difference between *a chicken* and *chicken*. Many nouns in English can be both countable and uncountable, depending on whether we are thinking in terms of units or of mass. By highlighting the difference using the same noun but with or without an article, the exercise aims to sensitize students to an important function of the article system in English.

Answers

1 1   Pat Smith
   2   Robin MacDonald
   3   Kim Patel
   4   Jo Brown
   5   Chris O'Connor

2   Other words that can be either countable or uncountable, but with a change of meaning are:

chocolate	a chocolate
beer	a beer
fish	a fish
potato	a potato
egg	an egg
stone	a stone
wood	a wood
light	a light

Consciousness-raising: Task Sheet 2

1 Look at the pictures, read the sentences and work out the name (first name and family name) of each person.

The person who ordered chicken is called Chris.
The person who has long hair is called Kim.
The person who bought a coffee is called Robin.
The person who is standing on a glass is called Jo.
The person who is eating ice cream is called Pat.
The family name of the person who has a long hair is Smith.
The family name of the person who is eating an ice cream is Brown.
The family name of the person who ordered a chicken is MacDonald.
The family name of the person who bought coffee is O'Connor.
The family name of the person who is standing on glass is Patel.

2 Now, check that you know the difference between:

chicken	a chicken
hair	a hair
coffee	a coffee
glass	a glass
ice cream	an ice cream

Can you add any more words to these lists? For example:

paper	a paper

Consciousness-raising: Task Sheet 3 (p105)
Passives – grammar interpretation task

As in Consciousness-raising: Task Sheet 2, students match pictures with sentences. The first part is receptive – students are challenged to understand the difference between the two sentences. In the second part they produce sentences, demonstrating their control over the difference between active and passive forms. Purists would argue that the production stage should be delayed at least until students have had a chance to notice this feature in naturally-occurring (or ungraded) input.

Answers

1 1 b)   2 b)   3 a)   4 a)   5 a)   6 a)

2 1   The man bit a snake. *Or* The snake was bitten by a man.
    2   The elephant frightened the mouse. *Or* The mouse was frightened by the elephant.
    3   The mother was fed by the child. *Or* The child fed the mother.
    4   The detective was followed by the woman. *Or* The woman followed the detective.
    5   The professor was driven to the university.
    6   This dog was bitten!

Consciousness-raising: Task Sheet 4 (p106)
Trends – grammar interpretation

This task targets a variety of tense and aspect distinctions which are represented visually as lines on a graph. In order to match the graph with its description students will need to recognize clues such as the fact that past tense signals a *break* with the present (*Recently pollution levels fell*) whereas the present perfect signals a *connection* with the present (*Recently pollution levels have fallen*).

Answers

1 1   Crime   5   Home ownership
    2   Unemployment   6   Tourism
    3   Heart disease   7   Population
    4   Birth rate   8   Infant mortality

Suggested answers

2 1   The population rose steadily during the seventies and has remained the same since then.
    2   The crime rate fell sharply during the early seventies and has been rising steadily since then.
    3   The number of people owning their own homes rose dramatically between 1970 and 1985 and has been falling gradually since then.
    4   The birth rate rose sharply during the seventies, then fell dramatically until 1990 and has been rising steadily since then.

Consciousness-raising: Task Sheet 3

1 Choose the sentence that goes with the picture.

a) The man bit a snake.
b) The man was bitten by a snake.

a) The elephant frightened the mouse.
b) The elephant was frightened by the mouse.

a) The mother fed the child.
b) The mother was fed by the child.

a) The detective followed the woman.
b) The detective was followed.

a) The professor drove to the university.
b) The professor was driven to the university.

a) This dog bites!
b) This dog was bitten!

2 Now, write sentences to go with these pictures.

Photocopiable

Consciousness-raising: Task Sheet 4

1 Read this information about an imaginary city and look at the graphs. Decide which graph represents which topic (Population, Crime, etc).

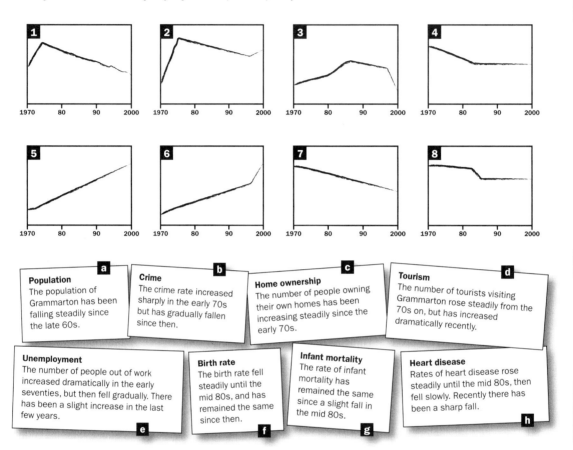

a Population
The population of Grammarton has been falling steadily since the late 60s.

b Crime
The crime rate increased sharply in the early 70s but has gradually fallen since then.

c Home ownership
The number of people owning their own homes has been increasing steadily since the early 70s.

d Tourism
The number of tourists visiting Grammarton rose steadily from the 70s on, but has increased dramatically recently.

e Unemployment
The number of people out of work increased dramatically in the early seventies, but then fell gradually. There has been a slight increase in the last few years.

f Birth rate
The birth rate fell steadily until the mid 80s, and has remained the same since then.

g Infant mortality
The rate of infant mortality has remained the same since a slight fall in the mid 80s.

h Heart disease
Rates of heart disease rose steadily until the mid 80s, then fell slowly. Recently there has been a sharp fall.

2 Now, write sentences about another city, using the information in these graphs:

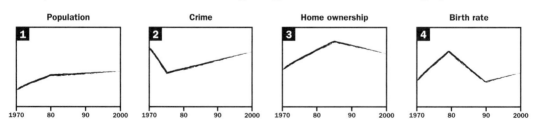

3 • Draw some graphs yourself about, for example, changes in fashion, in health, in leisure habits, in business or economy, in beliefs, in habits, etc in your local area or in some imaginary country.

• Write sentences to describe them, but in a different order.

• Exchange your graphs and sentences with other students. Can they match the sentence with the graph?

Consciousness-raising: Task Sheet 5 (p108)
Ergative verbs – grammar interpretation

This task, based on an idea by Rod Ellis, focuses on a feature of a large class of verbs in English that can be used transitively (ie with an object) and also intransitively (without an object) as in *Jack broke the window* and *The window broke*. Transitive verbs can also form passive constructions, giving a third way of expressing the same idea: *The window was broken by Jack*. This area presents a lot of problems for students, who tend to mix these structures to produce *Jack was break the window*, *The window was broke*, etc. The choice of either the transitive or the intransitive construction also allows the speaker to imply a greater or lesser degree of agency, hence responsibility: consider the difference between *I broke the window* and *The window broke*.

Answers

  1 c)
  2 j)
  3 f)
  4 d)
  5 h)
  6 b)
  7 i)
  8 e)
  9 a)
 10 g)

Consciousness-raising: Task Sheet 5

1   **Match these pictures with the correct sentences.**

a) The glass broke.
b) He broke the glass.
c) The door opened.
d) Someone opened the door.
e) The boat sank.

f) The boat was sunk by a whale.
g) The cat drowned.
h) The cat was drowned.
i) The car started.
j) She started the car.

2   **Look at the pictures again and cover the sentences. Can you remember the sentence for each picture? Choose from these structures.**

noun + active verb (The glass broke.)
noun + active verb + noun (Someone opened the door.)
noun + passive verb (The cat was drowned.)

3   **Look at this short dialogue.**
'The lock is broken! Did you break it?'
'No, it just broke.'

Write similar dialogues starting with these prompts.
1   The washing machine has stopped!
2   The toast is burnt!
3   The butter has melted!
4   The sink is blocked up!
5   The computer has shut down!
6   The car has stalled!
7   The mirror is cracked!
8   The sheets are torn!
9   The balloons have burst!

Chapter 8   **Grammar emergence tasks**

This set of tasks focuses on the principles outlined in Chapters 4 and 5, specifically the notion that grammar is an emergent phenomenon, and that the teacher's task, therefore, is not to *cover grammar* but to provide activities that allow the learners' emergent grammar to be rolled back, or *uncovered*. As a general principle, we suggested that classroom teaching needs to consist of cycles of input, output and feedback.

The input can come from a variety of sources, including the teacher's own talk. What is important is that some attention be given to both the language items and the language patterns in the input – traditionally a focus on words and on grammar, although this rigid distinction has started to look increasingly more fuzzy. Accordingly, some of the tasks below are directed at drawing attention to features of the input: they are *input enhancement* tasks, and these can be adapted to any material you choose.

Output and feedback tasks include the category of tasks called *reconstruction* tasks – that is, tasks in which students reconstruct a text and then compare it with the original. This comparison stage provides the feedback. Reconstruction tasks include dictogloss and retranslation activities. Again, the teacher is not limited by the choice of texts – any texts will do, so long as they are short and pitched at a level within the students' ability to understand but a little bit beyond their ability to produce with 100% accuracy. The examples in the tasks that follow should serve as a model.

Grammar emergence: Task Sheet 1 (pp110–11) Word list to text

This task is a text reconstruction task, but with a particular focus on vocabulary. The text is first 'reduced' to a list of words. (This is easily done using text processing software such as *Wordsmith Tools* (Oxford University Press).) The wordlist can be used as an aid to item learning, as well as a tool for reconstructing the text.

Answers

5   Words that go into these categories include:

Astronomy	Light	Movement
sky	bright	falling
stars	streaks (?)	streaks
meteors	glowing	trails
Earth	burn	shoot
atmosphere	flash	
	light	

Grammar emergence: Task Sheet 1

1 Fold your paper along the dotted line so you cannot see the text below.

The following list of words consists of *all* the words in the text, including the number of times each word appears. Check you know the meanings of all the words – use a dictionary, talk to a classmate or ask the teacher. What do you think the text is about?

A	1	GLOWING	1	NIGHTS	1	STREAKS	1
ACTUALLY	1	IN	2	OF	3	THE	3
ARE	1	LIGHT	1	ON	1	THESE	1
AS	1	LIKE	1	OR	1	THEY	3
ATMOSPHERE	1	LOOK	1	PART	1	THOUGH	1
BRIGHT	1	LUMPS	1	ROCK	1	THROUGH	1
BURN	1	MADE	1	SEE	1	TRAILS	1
BY	1	MAY	1	SHOOT	1	UP	1
EARTH'S	1	METAL	1	SKY	1	UPPER	1
FALLING	1	METEOR	1	SOME	1	YOU	1
FLASH	1	METEORS	1	STARS	1		

2 Now, look at the complete text at the bottom of the page. Were you right?

3 Now, cover the text, and, using the list of words, see if you can reconstruct the text. Use the grid below: each line represents a word. The 'grammar' words have been put in for you.

....

On some .... you may ....

in the .... Though they .... like ....

.... , these .... are ....

.... by .... , ... of .... or

.... As they .... through the ....

.... of the .... they .... up in

a .... of ....

4 Check your answers by comparing your text with the original.

5 Make three lists of words under these categories, using words from the text.
Astronomy   **Light**   **Movement**

fold here   *fold here*

Here is the complete text.

Meteor

On some nights you may see bright streaks in the sky. Though they look like falling stars, these glowing trails are actually made by meteors, lumps of rock or metal. As they shoot through the upper part of the Earth's atmosphere they burn up in a flash of light.

110

6 Fold your paper over again.

Here is another text, turned into a word list. What is the title of the text? Can you make any likely sentences using the words in the list? (The text consists of four sentences plus a one-word title.)

AFRICAN	1	CHAMELEON	2	ITSELF	1	THEIR	1
ANGRY	1	CHAMELEONS	1	LIZARDS	1	THEY	1
ARE	1	CHANGE	1	LONG	1	THIS	1
AS	1	COLOUR	1	MATCH	1	TO	2
BACKGROUND	1	DOES	1	OR	1	TONGUES	1
BY	1	INSECTS	1	OUT	1	WHEN	1
CAMOUFLAGE	1	IS	1	PROTECT	1		
CAN	1	IT	2	SHOOTING	1		
CATCH	1	ITS	1	THE	1		

7 Here is the text. This time the small 'grammar' words are missing. Can you complete the text?

Chameleon

Chameleons .... African lizards. .... catch insects ....
shooting .... long tongues. .... chameleon
.... change colour .... match .... background.
.... does .... camouflage, ... protect
.... , ... when .... angry.

fold here   *fold here*

- -

8 Now read the complete text.

Chameleon

Chameleons are African lizards. They catch insects by shooting out their long tongues. The chameleon can change colour to match its background. It does this as camouflage, to protect itself, or when it is angry.

9 Look at the word list for CHAMELEON. Can you put any of the words into groups of related meanings?

Grammar emergence: Task Sheet 2 (p113)
Pattern detection task – poem

The ability to detect patterns in language is fundamental to successful, self-directed learning. A good way to start is by looking for patterns in text that is highly patterned, often in a very obvious way, as is the case with a lot of poetry.

Answers

2   Words that appear twice or more are: *the* (7), *and* (6), *I* (4), *she* (4), *love* (3), *my* (3), *on* (3), and: *as, bid, but, by, did, easy, foolish, gardens, her, me, salley, snow-white, take, with, young* (each twice).

3   Word families (there is some overlap):
parts of the body: *shoulder, hand, feet*
movement: *passed, meet, stand, leaning, laid*
gardens: *salley, gardens, leaves, tree, grow*
countryside: *field, river, grass, weirs*
youth: *young, foolish*
coercion: *bid, (not) agree*

4   Possible patterns:
[place adverbial] + [place adverbial]
down	*by the salley gardens*
in a field	*by the river*

[noun phrase] + [verb, emphatic form]
my love and I	*did meet*
my love and I	*did stand*

she bid me take   **[noun phrase]**   *easy*
she bid me take	*love*	*easy*
she bid me take	*life*	*easy*

as +   **[noun phrase] +**   *grow(s) +*   **[preposition phrase]**
as	*the leaves*	*grow*	*on the tree*
as	*the grass*	*grows*	*on the weirs*

but I   **[verb to be]**   **young and foolish**
but I	*being*	*young and foolish*
but I	*was*	*young and foolish*

5   A prose reworking of the poem might be:
My love and I met down by the salley gardens. She passed the salley gardens with little snow-white feet. She bid me take love easy, as the leaves grow on the tree. But I, being young and foolish, would not agree with her. My love and I stood in a field by the river, and she laid her snow-white hand on my leaning shoulder. She bid me take life easy, as the grass grows on the weirs. But I was young and foolish, and now am full of tears.
The poetic effects are mainly in word order, with a preference for using preposition phrases to begin sentences, and use of emphatic auxiliaries *(did stand).*

6   Many of the repeated patterns have been identified in the preceding exercises. Things to note are the way each stanza accumulates detail but then, in the fourth line, introduces a contrast with *but*. Note also how each stanza moves through a pattern of *we (my love and I)*, *she* and finally *I* – perhaps indicative of the loneliness experienced by the poet. What is also significant is the way the story is told in the past, but in the very last line moves into the present, breaking the pattern of the first stanza: *and now am full of tears.*

Grammar emergence: Task Sheet 2

1 Read this poem.

> ### Down by the salley gardens
>
> Down by the salley gardens my love and I did meet;
> She passed the salley gardens with little snow-white feet.
> She bid me take love easy, as the leaves grow on the tree;
> But I, being young and foolish, with her would not agree.
>
> In a field by the river my love and I did stand,
> And on my leaning shoulder she laid her snow-white hand.
> She bid me take life easy, as the grass grows on the weirs;
> But I was young and foolish, and now am full of tears.
> *William Butler Yeats*

Note
salley: small tree cultivated for basket making
bid: literary word meaning *asked, invited*
weir: a wall built across a river, under the water

2 Make a list of all the words that appear more than once in the poem. To help you, here are the most frequent words.
the (7)   *and* (6)   *I* (4)   *she* (4)

3 *Shoulder* and *hand* belong to the same word family. How many more word families can you find in the poem?

4 *She bid me take love easy* and *She bid me take life easy* are the same pattern of words almost exactly repeated. Can you find other examples of pattern repetition in the poem?

5 Rewrite the poem as prose:
My love and I met....

What patterns disappear when you turn the poem into prose? In other words, what patterns are particularly poetic?

6 Compare the first four lines of the poem (ie the first stanza) and the second four lines (the second stanza). In what way are they the same and in what way different? For example, look at the way the first three lines of stanza 1 add to each other, but then the fourth line begins with *but*. Is the same true in the second stanza? And what about the subjects of each line: *my love and I*; *she*; *she*; *I*?

Grammar emergence: Task Sheet 3 (p115)
Pattern detection task – prose

In the preceding task we saw how a poem is patterned – at the level of words, sentence patterns and text organization. This task looks at a piece of factual writing, again looking for patterns at each of these levels.

Answers

1   The text is an advertisement for a charity; its purpose is *to appeal for help.*

2   a)   repeated words: *a* (5), *will* (4), *be* (3), *Christmas* (3), *dogs* (3), *the* (3); *and, by, dumped, like, Jake, many, N.C.D.L., of* (each 2).

    b)   synonyms: *injured, sick; rescue, save; refuge, home; provide, help*

    c)   antonyms: *sick - healthy; destroy - save; dumped - saved; thousands - single*

    d)   *puppies, dogs, animal*   *injured, sick, healthy*
        safe, save, saved   *dumped, destroy, cruelly*
        Christmas, presents, give,   *rescue, refuge, save, loving, home*
        seasonal, festivities

3   a)   repeated phrase: *dogs like Jake*

    b)   *dumped at CHRISTMAS, saved by the N.C.DL.*
        will be given, will be [...] dumped;
        we won't [will not] destroy, we'll provide

    c)   the division of the text into two paragraphs reflects the two-part title: *DUMPED AT CHRISTMAS* summarizes the gist of the first paragraph; *SAVED BY THE N.C.D.L.* summarizes the second. This structure in turn reflects a problem – solution organization, one which is common to a great many text types.

5   1   The text is a news story, written to inform and, perhaps, partly to amuse.

    2   a)   repeated words: grammatical words, such as *the, in, a, his, of, and, at, was* are repeated, but are of less interest than the repeated lexical words *(black, doing, man police, raindance, spotting/spotted, call/called)*, which capture the gist of the story better.

        b)   synonyms: *stunned, worried, baffled; villagers, locals, residents; nut, crackpot, oddball; weird, bizarre; claimed, admitted.*

        c)   antonyms: no obvious ones, but there is clearly a polarity between *locals, villagers, residents* (on the one hand) and *nut, crackpot, oddball* (on the other).

        d)   *witch-doctor, raindance, ritual;*   *arms, chest, mouth*
            leaping, waving   *boots, nail varnish, tattoos*

    3   a)   repeated phrases: *doing a raindance; doing some kind of raindance*

        b)   *spotting a ... witch-doctor doing; reporting the man doing; the man... was spotted leaping...* All follow a verb + noun + verb + *ing* pattern.
            Also: *stunned villagers, worried locals, baffled police:* the pattern is participle + noun.

        c)   The last sentence is a re-phrasing of the first sentence, and includes all the actors: *police, villagers, the man/witch-doctor,* as well as the activities: *calling and doing a rain-dance.* Notice that the kind of verbs associated with the villagers and the police are what are sometimes called verbs of *mental* and *verbal processes* (spotting, called, claimed, reporting, admitted), whereas the verbs associated with the man are *action processes: doing, leaping, waving, foaming* – the dynamic nature of these processes is further emphasised by the use of the progressive aspect (-ing) throughout. The combined effect is to portray the villagers/police as passive observers and reporters of an alien, rather frenzied activity - this pattern ripples though every sentence of the text.

Grammar emergence: Task Sheet 3

1 **Read the following text and decide**

a) what kind of text it is – eg news story, letter, advertisement...

b) what its purpose is – eg to warn, to inform, to criticize...

DUMPED AT CHRISTMAS – SAVED BY THE N.C.D.L.

In a few weeks, thousands of dogs like Jake will be given as Christmas presents. Yet many of them will be cruelly dumped once the seasonal festivities are over. Young puppies and dogs - many injured and sick - will flood the N.C.D.L.'s Rescue Centres.

But **we won't** destroy a single healthy animal. We'll simply provide a safe refuge until a loving new home can be found. Will you help save more dogs like Jake this Christmas by making a donation today?

2 *Word patterns*

In the text find examples of

a) repetition (ie words that are repeated)

b) synonyms (ie words with similar meaning)

c) antonyms (ie words with opposite meaning)

d) word families (ie words that are related by meaning, such as *puppies, dogs* or by form, such as *safe, save*)

3 *Phrase and sentence patterns*

In the text find examples of

a) phrases that are repeated

b) grammatical structures that are repeated

c) any other evidence you think might be a pattern

4 **You are going to try to reconstruct the text from memory. But before you do, you can write down a maximum of ten words to help you. When you have selected your ten words, cover the text and try to reconstruct it.**

5 **Here is another text. Repeat tasks 1, 2 and 3.**

RAIN DANCE NUT SCARES VILLAGERS WITH WEIRD RITUAL

Stunned villagers called police after spotting a crackpot weekend witch-doctor doing a rain dance in an empty field.

The man, in his late 20s, was spotted leaping about in a pair of winkle-picker boots and waving his arms in the air.

Worried locals in Bretby, near Derby, claimed the oddball was sporting black nail varnish and had black Chinese-style tattoos all over his bare chest. At the height of the bizarre ritual, he even began foaming at the mouth.

Baffled police admitted: 'We received a call from residents reporting the man doing some kind of rain dance.'

6 **Now reconstruct the text. This time you can choose 15 words for your 'notes'.**

Photocopiable

Grammar emergence: Task Sheet 4 (pp117–8)
Pattern detection task – multiple texts

Patterns are easier to detect the more often they appear, and one way of sensitizing learners to the patterns of text is to provide multiple examples of the same text type. By comparing the different examples, learners can do a lot of the detective work themselves. Note that it helps if these texts are short, so as to reduce the reading load. There are a wide variety of text types that are good for this purpose: horoscopes, advertisements, 'news in brief' items, TV guide film summaries, instructions, weather forecasts, etc.

Answers

1   The text in this task is from a brochure issued by a bank warning its customers to take care of their credit cards.

2   Words belonging to the categories include:

Money	Crime	Inconvenience
(credit/cheque) card	burgled	embarrassing
spent	break-in	irritating
£500	stolen/stole	angry
wallet	thief/thieves	a real pain
cash	snatch	stupidly
cheques	robbed	hassle
cash machines		a real fool
debit/credit payments		
pay		

3   1   it's irritating to think
     2   it was a real pain
     3   he couldn't pay / I couldn't write cheques
     4   the locks had to be changed
     5   someone had spent / I had [never] been / I had been robbed

4   The overall structure consists of:
   - a short dramatic headline (*Burgled; Car Break-In*)
   - circumstantial information in the third person: names, places and a complicating event
   - a direct speech account by the victim of the consequences of the crime, including the amount of inconvenience caused.

5   This text has a different function from the bank brochure text. The purpose of the newspaper text is to inform, rather than warn, and hence it omits the first person accounts and the inconvenience language. It is more like an itemized list taken from police records. This demonstrates how the function of a text shapes its organization.

Grammar emergence: Task Sheet 4

1 The following four texts all come from a brochure. Read the texts and decide a) who sent the brochure? b) what was the purpose of the brochure?

IT HAPPENED TO ME

Burgled: Peter Carson is retired. His home was recently broken into. His next credit card bill surprised him.

'Someone had spent almost £500 in electrical shops I had never been to. I suppose my card was stolen from the house along with everything else.

I only use my card occasionally, so I didn't realize my card was gone for two months. It was embarrassing to have to tell the bank so long after the event.

It's irritating to think I gave the thief money on a plate.'

IT HAPPENED TO ME

Car Break-In: Steven and Janet Robertson went for a Sunday walk. Steven left his wallet in the car glove compartment thinking it would be safe.

'I was really angry. Mainly with the thieves who stole all my cards and cash, but also with myself for leaving them in the car.

I've installed a car alarm now and I'll make sure that I never leave my wallet in the car again. I couldn't write cheques, use cash machines or make any debit or credit payments. It was a real pain.'

IT HAPPENED TO ME

Shop Snatch: Carol Adams was shopping for clothes, when her bag was stolen.

'I put my bag on the floor, turned away for thirty seconds, and it was taken. Stupidly I'd put my cheque card in with my cheque book. My cash, credit card, house keys, diary and address book all went as well.

I had to make several calls, cancelling cards and cheques. The locks had to be changed on my front door. I couldn't remember appointments and telephone numbers. It took ages to sort everything out. It was so much hassle.'

IT HAPPENED TO ME

Pub Grab: Mick Wilson met his friends in a pub on a hot Saturday night. He hung his jacket over his shoulder, and when it came to his round, he found he couldn't pay.

'I felt a real fool, in front of all my mates. The laughter died down when they realized I had been robbed. I lost £50 in cash, my season ticket and all my cards.

I spent the rest of my Saturday night at the police station and on the phone, rather than having fun.'

---

2 Find words in the texts that belong to these families:

Money   **Crime**   **Inconvenience**

3 **Find other examples in the text of these patterns:**

1 *It* + verb *to be* + adjective + *to* + infinitive
   eg It was embarrassing to have to tell the bank...

2 *It* + verb *to be* + NP (noun phrase)
   eg It was so much hassle.

3 NP + *couldn't* + infinitive
   eg I couldn't remember...

4 NP + *had* + *to* + infinitive
   eg I had to make...

5 NP + *had* + past participle
   eg I'd put...

4 **Compare the structure of the four texts: what do they have in common? For example, the first paragraph of each text is different from the rest of the text. In what way? And why?**

5 **Here is a news item about a crime. In what way is it different to the four texts on the previous page? Why do you think it is different?**

Assaults blight weekend
Police kept busy

Monday, 15 May

A string of late night and early morning assaults and thefts from cars were dealt with by Masterton police at the weekend.

Two cars were broken into on Saturday, with a camera worth over £1000 taken from a car parked on Sussex Street. A handbag was stolen from a car parked behind Food For Thought and was later found with a Visa card taken from it. On Sunday a handbag was taken from a car parked in the council car park on Lincoln Road, and a sports bag was taken from a car parked outside the Horseshoe Tavern. The bag and rugby boots were later found behind a building on Dixon Street.

6 **Have you ever been robbed? Or do you know someone who has? Write the story in the style of the texts in exercise 1 (IT HAPPENED TO ME). Don't forget to emphasize the inconvenience!**

Grammar emergence: Task Sheet 5 (pp120–21)
Texts for retranslation and dictogloss

In Chapter 5 we saw how texts can be used for reconstruction tasks, specifically dictogloss and retranslation. Here is a collection of texts that can be used for these purposes. These may help you get an idea as to what kind of texts are suitable. Small narratives, such as jokes, work well. So do short poems, because of their inherent repetition and (sometimes) rhyme. Note that it is important that a) the texts are complete and b) the texts are very short: a maximum of 50 words is a good rule of thumb.

The basic procedure for dictogloss is the following:

- Tell the class to listen to the text and not to write. Tell them that the object of the exercise is to remember any words or expressions they can and to write them down as soon as you have finished reading.
- Write the title of the text (if it has one) and any proper names in it on the board. Tell students what kind of text it is, eg poem, joke, etc.
- Read the text once, clearly and at a natural speed.
- Give students a non-verbal signal to start writing, individually.
- Tell students to work in pairs or threes, and, using their notes, to try to reconstruct the text from memory.
- Once they have attempted this, and if it is feasible, put them into larger groups to compare notes and to alter their texts if necessary. It may be helpful to read the text again at this stage.
- Elicit the complete text on to the board, writing on one half of the board only; alternatively, appoint a class 'secretary' to do the board writing.
- Read out the original text, or, using an OHP, project it on to the blank half of the board. Ask students to identify any differences between the 'class text' and the original. These differences may indicate gaps in their language knowledge.

Variations of the dictogloss approach include the following:

- Instead of reading the text, allow students briefly to see the text by, for example, projecting it using an OHP. They then reconstruct it from memory.
- As you read (or tell) the text to the class, record yourself. Go back to the recording at the checking stage.

The basic procedure for retranslation is:

- Students read the text (in English) and – working individually, in pairs or small groups – freely translate it into their own language.
- The original text is then covered up or removed, and, using their translation, they retranslate it back into English.
- They then compare their retranslation with the original English text, identifying any differences. As with dictogloss, these differences may indicate gaps in their language knowledge.

Variation

- The class is divided into an even number of groups with two or three students in each group. Half of the groups are given a short text in English to translate into the mother tongue. The other half does the same with a second text of similar type and length. The groups then exchange their translations and attempt to render them back into English (not having seen the original text on which the translation is based). They are then shown the originals and make comparisons.

Grammar emergence: Task Sheet 5

1 Poems

THE ACT

There were the roses, in the rain.
Don't cut them, I pleaded.
      They won't last, she said.
But they're so beautiful
      where they are.
Agh, we were all beautiful once, she
      said,
and cut them and gave them to me
      in my hand.

(William Carlos Williams)

WALKING AT DUSK

Wonderful long evenings!
I walk slowly about, carrying an old stick.
The moon calms its part of the sky.
White clouds roll and do not move.
The cows seem to be growing out of the
   field.

(Robert Bly)

HIGH COUNTRY WEATHER

Alone we are born
      And die alone;
Yet see the red-gold cirrus
      Over snow-mountain shine.

Upon the upland road
      Ride easy, stranger:
Surrender to the sky
      Your heart of anger.

(James K. Baxter)

OVER THE FIELDS

Over the sky, the clouds are moving,
Over the fields, the wind is blowing,
Over the fields the lost child
Of my mother is wandering.

Over the street, leaves are falling,
Over the trees, birds are crying -
Over the mountains, far away,
My home must be.

(Hermann Hesse)

2 News items

Dolphin Saves Boy From Drowning

A dolphin saved a 14-year-old boy from drowning. The boy, who could not swim, fell from the boat as he was sailing with his father. As he was slipping under the water, something pushed him up. The dolphin carried the boy to the boat and swam away.

Parrot Gets Parking Ticket

A traffic policeman in a Greek town decided that a parrot was blocking the pavement so he gave it a ticket. The parrot was placed outside a pet shop on a stand every morning by his owner. Greek television showed the owner handing the ticket to the parrot, who tore it up.

3 Jokes

A penguin walks into a bar, looking worried. He goes up to the bar and asks the barman, 'Have you seen my brother?' The barman asks, 'What does he look like?'

A hippopotamus walks into a bar and asks the barman for a beer. 'That will be ten dollars, please,' says the barman. So the hippo gives the barman his money and starts to drink his beer. 'You know, we don't get very many hippos in here,' the barman comments. The hippo replies, 'At these prices I'm not surprised!'

A man driving in the outback sees a farmer staggering from tree to tree carrying a huge emu. The emu is eating acorns from the trees. He stops the car and says, 'Why don't you put the emu down and shake the tree? Then the acorns will fall down and that would save a lot of time.' The man says, 'What's time to an emu?'

4 Urban legends, anecdotes

A Yorkshire family was sitting down to tea and slicing up the bread for chip butties. Father cut a slice that seemed to have a small black mark in the centre. The mark got bigger with each slice, until the stunned family could gradually make out the shape of a dead mouse baked into the loaf.

An office worker ran out of cash during an evening's drinking and, needing some money for a taxi home, went to a cash dispenser. He slipped in his card, the glass started to go up, and two startled pigeons flew out.

A Royal Air Force airman was surprised to receive notice that he was to be discharged from the service. He was even more surprised when he read the reason - he was pregnant! The computer had made an error.

Caroline McKenna was working in the Shop Inn, Wokingham, in southern England, when two firemen rushed in and asked to use the telephone. They called the fire brigade to come out urgently - their fire engine was on fire!

In 1956, the opera singer, Hans Hotter, strode out on to the stage of the Royal Opera House, London, during Act Three of Die Walküre. He was greeted by roars of laughter. He had been in such a rush to put on his cloak, he had not noticed the coat hanger sticking out of his collar!

121

Photocopiable

Index